Teaching Asperger's Students Social Skills Through Acting

All Their World's a Stage!

Amelia Davies

Teaching Asperger's Students Social Skills Through Acting

All marketing and publishing rights guaranteed to and
reserved by

FUTURE HORIZONS INC.

721 W. Abram Street
Arlington, Texas 76013
800-489-0727
817-277-0727
817-277-2270 (fax)
E-mail: info@futurehorizons-autism.com
www.FutureHorizons-autism.com

Printed in the United States of America.

Cataloging in Publications Data is available from the Library
of Congress.

ISBN 1-932565-11-6

Table of Contents

Dedication

I wrote this book for all the people I met during conferences who looked at me wistfully and said "I wish I was talented enough to do that stuff." Well, you are, you can, and you will!

Foreword

Actors study people. They study what people do and say, how they look and act when they are feeling different feelings or thinking different thoughts. It is a necessity of the actor's profession that they spy on people, listening for nuances in tone of voice and looking for subtle cues in facial expression and body language that give away what people are thinking, feeling, and intending. They take what they have learned about these non-verbal cues to the stage, and the better they are at mimicking others, the better their art.

So what does this have to do with Asperger's Syndrome and autism? It turns out that some very advanced people with Asperger's Syndrome naturally do the same thing. They recognize that they are missing out on social language and on the myriad of unspoken, unwritten social rules that govern how people get along with each other, and they instinctively start to study other people's interactions in order to learn those non-verbal cues and mysterious rules. It also turns out that some individuals with Asperger's Syndrome become so good at this that they end up becoming professional actors, sometimes even famous actors. Through repeated observation and practice, these folks presumably use other cognitive areas of the brain to take over the work of the parts of the brain that typically process social-emotional and communication information. People in this sub-group of individuals with autism disorders instinctively have found a method to help them understand social-emotional exchanges. However, even the most able among them typically still lag behind in their social development, and they may go through their childhood and teenage years always trying to catch up, but never seeming to quite fit in. This is where drama classes come in. We use drama to speed up the natural learning process in individuals who have already begun to study non-verbal communication, and to introduce this process to those who have not.

Real help is there both for those people who already have begun to study non-verbal communication in real life situations and for those who have not. People with autism need to have social skills slowed down and broken down into small steps in order to learn. This type of social learning can happen in a social skills group or in one-on-one sessions with a teacher or mentor. It can also happen in acting class.

So what happens in a typical acting class? In class, the teacher typically uses an assortment of exercises to teach discrete acting skills.

These skills include the use of body language and movement, facial expression, and tone of voice. When one considers that probably somewhere between seventy and eighty percent of what we communicate is passed on to other people not through our words but through non-verbal cues, it is readily apparent why actors spend so much time studying these cues. Acting exercises break down these non-verbal skills into small, structured steps. The complexity and pace of subsequent steps increases until eventually the actor is ready to prepare for a performance. The key here is that the actor practices each necessary skill before being expected to put it all together on stage. Likewise, people with autism need to have social-emotional skills broken down into small, distinct skills upon which they can later build more complex skills. It is critical to recognize that in order to achieve the best possible outcome in real-life social situations, people on the autism spectrum need to first practice social skills in controlled environments. Acting classes provide a ready-made setting for this type of practice.

People with higher-functioning autism are the perfect candidates for acting classes. These individuals need to learn to recognize and portray social-emotional cues in real-life. These are skills that are crucial to understanding what other people are thinking, feeling, and intending during social exchanges. Acting classes teach these very skills. Without these abilities, the chances are high that our friends, students, and loved ones with autism will fare poorly at holding down rewarding jobs, making close friends, or having intimate relationships.

The difference between an acting student with autism and one without is that the stakes are much higher for the person with autism. A professional actor can choose a new career if things don't work out, whereas a person with autism is not likely to be able to opt out on social interactions as long as he or she wants to have a family, friends, and career. Even given optimal help with social-emotional skills, most individuals with autism face times when they simply cannot process social exchanges rapidly enough to keep up. At times like this, they sometimes fall back on using a previously practiced role until they can catch up. Acting lessons designed for individuals with higher functioning autism can help prepare our students for times like these.

So who can teach a drama class for students with autism? With a little guidance any interested, committed person can. This is where *Teaching Asperger's Students Social Skills Through Acting* comes in. Amelia Davies has written a wonderful book for anyone, even for those without drama expertise—who would like to teach social skills through the medium of theater arts. For the past three years I have had the uncommonly good fortune of working with Amelia in using drama to teach social and communication skills to children and adults with higher functioning autism. Amelia is a remarkably talented and contagiously funny actress and teacher. She received her Bachelor's of Fine Arts from Boston Conservatory, and her Master's of Fine Arts in acting from Brandeis University. She then made her living for many years as an actress, director, and producer, including a national tour with the Missoula Children's Theatre. Drawing both on her background in theatre and on her experience working with adults and children with autism, Amelia has developed a fun, easy to follow, step-by-step drama curriculum specifically for parents and professionals without backgrounds in acting. The short plays at the end of the book (written by Amelia's amazing husband, John Stamm) are all take-offs of children's fairy tales. Stamm's sense of humor simmers throughout each play, and audience members are sure to have a memorable time when they see the final production.

Jeanie McAfee, M.D.
March 15, 2004

Acknowledgements

Thank you to Dr. Jeanie McAfee, the Goddess of Social Skills, and the wild McAfee clan for inviting me into their lives and teaching me all their wonderful lessons. Knowing you is an exhilarating and life shaping experience.

Thank you to Future Horizons for being excited about this book when I was still biting my nails over it.

Thank you to Lynn Arp and Krista Raj for keeping me sane and always answering their phones.

Thank you to my wonderful group of acting students, who always make me laugh.

Thank you to my English classes at Yuba City High School, my friends in the English Department, and Bill Zeller.

Thank you to my Moms, Joan Davies and Susan Parry, for never letting me get away with less that my best.

Finally, thank you to John Stamm, my husband, my Mighty-Man, with whom every moment is wicked good.

Introduction

Worried that you don't know enough about acting to understand this book? Think you need some sort of magical talent to make the exercises in this book work? Convinced that only certain people can pull off a drama class or direct a play? Well, sorry to contradict you so soon in our relationship, but you are absolutely wrong. And believe me, I would let you know.

Now, if you want Oscar winning performances from perfectly behaved kids while you break new ground in the arts as the sun sets in the West, then quick, quick, quick, put this book down and go find a Fairy Godmother. And, if you want a serious and high powered social skills curriculum that drills kids in a predictable, structured and clearly defined environment, quick, quick, quick, put this book down.

Are you still holding on? Good.

Now, ask yourself these questions.

1. Do I have a sense of humor? (Tip: If you aren't sure, ask the person next to you to make a loud farting noise in a crowded area. Did you laugh? Yes? You're okay.)

2. Do I want to make this drama class thing work?

3. Do I believe that kids can benefit from a healthy dose of self-esteem, some training in the fine art of fitting in and at least five good belly laughs a week?

Yes, yes, YES? Great! You've already tackled the tough stuff.

But ... beware.

When teaching an acting class, you are your own student. You may find yourself adopting some of that fun and carefree behavior that you encourage in your acting class, a desire to (gasp) "wing it" and a tendency to tweak and modify everything in this book to fit your specific group of kids. When this happens, and you are still arriving to class on time, you will have struck the perfect balance. Hooray!

I'd love to tell you that all the exercises in this book are from my own brilliant mind. That I single-handedly discovered the link between the needs of beginning actors and those of Asperger's students studying social skills. That from the very first class I knew exactly what I was doing and I never made a mistake with my students. But the fact is, many of these exercises or "theater games" are standard first year acting drills.

If you know anyone with even a bit of acting training, they will confirm this. What I have been able to do is find links between the needs of beginning acting students and students with Asperger's Syndrome. As for the "never made a mistake" part, there were days when everything I planned to do fell flat and we had to just sit in a circle and get a grip on ourselves.

So now you're thinking,

Huh.

Why, then, should I use this book?

Well, I hope you will use it as a starting place. A springboard that you will use as a general guide. Because, believe me, every group of kids is different and you are the expert on that group.

If you are like me, you want to know a little about the person who is going to help you out. Here it goes, this is me.

I studied acting and directing with an emphasis on improvisational theater. I received both an undergraduate and graduate degrees in this field of study. I spent my twenties enjoying a terrific, exciting, self-supporting career in the theater; performing, directing and teaching classes. An extended bout of pneumonia coupled with a wish to collect my thoughts and get my second wind brought me to the Central Valley in California, where I landed a job as a high school

English teacher. I figured I'd stick around for a year, and then get back to business. I fell in love with teaching and decided to switch careers. Five years later, I was approached by the head of the Special Ed Department, who asked me if I was interested in tutoring a student with High Functioning Autism. Like many people who are unfamiliar with autism, I thought, Autism; *Rainman*. That was the extent of my knowledge. I knew that it was something I didn't know much about. Things like that always interest me. The school set up a meeting with the mother of the student whom I was to tutor. When I met Dr. Jeanie McAfee, I thought she was a bright, driven mother who was interested in the happiness of her child and who was kind enough to bring chocolate cake to our first meeting. I was right. What I didn't know was that she was a world famous authority on teaching social skills to students with Asperger's Syndrome and High Functioning Autism, author of that soon to be seminal book, *Navigating the Social World*. And it's a good thing too, because I might not have been so at ease. From the first, we got along well and agreed on the key points of her daughter Rachel's education in literature. So, I took the job and for the next month or so spent several hours a week tutoring Rachel.

One afternoon after a tutoring session, Jeanie said she wished she knew someone with some drama background because she wanted to find a way to blend theater games into her social skills sessions. I said I thought I might be who she was looking for. And the rest, as the cliché goes, is history. Jeanie told me what she wanted the kids to get out of class. I showed her my bag of tricks and we went from there.

I'm not a doctor. I'm not a Special Education teacher. I'm not a respite worker, O.T., or anything else that difficult. I'm an acting teacher. As far as I'm concerned, all my students are ACTING students. My classroom is an ACTING studio and the time spent in it is spent on learning highly classified ACTING secrets. Like, how to appear confident when you actually feel scared. How to hold someone's attention. How to make someone feel happy and comfortable. How to guess what people are thinking just by the way they hold their body.

I never mention social skills or Asperger's Syndrome. Sometimes my students do, but we don't dwell on it. In my opinion, these kids could use a break from their autism diagnosis. The only time I mention it is to tell them that because of their diagnosis, they have a predisposition to becoming talented actors. This is why, I tell them, I have hand picked them to be in my advanced acting class. And, as any actor, they will be working hard. I also explain to them that some of the things they will learn are TOP SECRET acting secrets, that typical, ordinary people aren't ready to hear.

Still there? Good. Now let's get started.

Part 1

Getting Started

We are creating a tight, exciting, exclusive little unit here. Not a class, but a club. A clique. A place to develop inside jokes and secret handshakes. A place that when all else fails, you can throw yourself on the ground, tell your story, and the rest of your acting buddies will commiserate and say— "Yeah, been there, done that."

The way to do this is to conduct the first three or four classes treating the students as one complete unit. A group. Refer to them as a group, praise them as a group, discuss problems as the problems of the group. No one is ever singled out for a response. They move as a group, listen as a group, make chicken noises as a group and eat cookies as a group.

Are big red flags going up in your head?

Do you hear the words "How in the heck will I get them to do that? MY kids with Asperger's Syndrome will NOT do that."

This is where being an ACTING TEACHER, not a SOCIAL SKILLS TEACHER can be very helpful. After all, you're not teaching a class full of Asperger's students, you're teaching a class full of fabulous actors! You "don't know" that Bobby hates Carl and Sierra can't stand when people make smacking noises with their lips and Peter isn't comfortable standing near people he doesn't know. Yes, it's a scary ledge to walk on but it's been my experience that if you expect a kid to do something, they'll do it if they possibly can. So, while it's unrealistic for your students to be able to physically interact in an invasive and complex way (as they would need to during a performance of a play) right off the bat, you can expect them to work towards becoming more socially comfortable.

Once you teach this class, you will be in on THE BIG SECRET! Students with Asperger's are frequently very talented actors. Many parents have told me that their child enjoys memorizing and performing sounds and voices, body movements and long passages from their favorite movies, TV shows and books. When I tell people that I am an acting teacher to students with High Functioning Autism, they often frequently adopt a concerned look and say, "Oh, how wonderful of you. That must be so difficult." Ha! I have taught many levels of acting, from beginner to advanced and I can honestly say that each class of Asperger's students has contained more charisma and raw talent than many of my collegiate or G.A.T.E. level classes. Every single one of my students has a well developed sense of humor. Some enjoy high energy, wacky slapstick, others possess a quirky, dry wit that livens up the quieter moments. I have often wondered if in addition to having common core deficits, Asperger's students might not also have been blessed with core assets, such as theatrical ability. When I first started to read about Asperger's Syndrome in preparation for development of my class curriculum, I was struck by the similarities I found between the descriptions of the behavior of people with Asperger's Syndrome and the behavior of several of the most talented actors I worked with in graduate school. Each of these actors possessed a rare and unique way of dealing with the world that made it difficult for them to relate to the rest of us in what we saw as a normal way. That same unique quality gave their performances an exquisite and beautiful ring of truth that cannot be taught. The society of artists is an accepting one, and people are embraced for who they are, not for who they should be. We just enjoyed these actors on their own terms and never thought another thing about it. If they were uncomfortable with eye contact or physical proximity, oh well. Their odd perceptions of social situations were taken as artistic perceptions and many times envied. Now, will every acting student of yours become a star? Maybe one of them will. Probably none of them will. But, it is worth it to note that these students tend to have aptitude in the very craft that attracts others who are most likely to accept and appreciate them. Here's a little list of what else you'll need to accomplish.

What You Need

- An indoor space, without nooks and crannies. (Tip: a regular theater is a nightmare in this situation. There are too many poorly lit nooks and crannies. You will lose your students in under five minutes and may never retrieve them.)

- An hour block of time, organized into fifty minutes of drama training and ten minutes of structured break time.

- Ten weeks of that scheduled hour.

- Permission to make A LOT of noise.

- A group of parents and student aides willing to follow you into the Land of Silly.

- Five to eight students with Asperger's Syndrome, High Functioning Autism or some other such thing.

Fill these requirements and your drama class will be a success. For those of you who are meticulous and organized, I've been much more specific elsewhere in the book. If it will make you feel better, thumb through the book and take a look at the exercise descriptions, letters to parents, even suggestions for student attire. Revel in all that detail and calm that little voice in your head that keeps demanding details.

Go Find

Occasionally, I have had adults tell me that no neurotypical child would ever be interested in being a helpful peer to a student with Asperger's Syndrome. They seem to be very convinced in this opinion and I wonder, do they actually KNOW any neurotypical children? Because it has been my experience that there are plenty of bright, empathetic neurotypical children out there just waiting to find some way of making a difference in their community. You just might not always recognize them right off the bat. Many people make the mistake of searching for their aides solely in the higher level or gifted classes at school. While there are many wonderful students to be found there, do not ignore the students less gifted in academics. Frequently, students who have not been successful in school due to learning or emotional disabilities make great mentors for younger students. They know what it's like to have difficulty grasping concepts or fitting in. Choosing these students as aides not only gives your Asperger's students great peer mentors, it gives the aides something to be good at, something to be proud of. During our first year of acting class, we had a young man as one of our aides. Apparently, this young man had been struggling in school and with some of the less than legal behavior he had chosen to indulge in. However, Jeanie saw something in his eye that made her want to give him a go. Thank goodness! He was a wonderful asset to our class. His strong presence and street cool demeanor made the little boys in our class adore him. They clung to him like barnacles. I was glad to see this, because so many of the people working in this kind of child care are women. Once, one of my many male students complained that he was being "girled to death." Often, when ADHD and the heat made our more active boys into wiggle worms, all we had to do was ask our young man to sit down next to the students who were being disruptive. All he had to do was give them a smile, and -BOOM- instant success where I would have had none.

Now, the story continues. I had this same young man as a student in my English class that next year. When I saw his name on my roster, I was delighted. But the young man who entered my classroom was hardly recognizable. Sullen and sporadically there, he was the butt of many derogatory comments from a class full of less than academically gifted students. He was failing, he was difficult and he was driving me up a wall. One day however, after being scolded for sleeping in class, he had apparently had enough of the teasing he received from his classmates, and responded to some obnoxious comment with "Hey, I am a teacher's aide. So shut up." Actually, he used language a bit more colorful than that. When the class saw that I not only ignored his vocabulary but confirmed his claim, they "shut up." I have lost track of this talented young man, but I hope that wherever he goes, he remembers the good work he did for me, and knows his own value.

Sometimes teachers will tell me that parents will not want their neurotypical children involved with students with Asperger's Syndrome, or any student with a learning disability, especially if it pulls them away from their regular class once in a while. Yes, it's hard to believe that people would say that, but in actuality, we have heard that type of thing from a group of educators in a close by college community that shall remain nameless, but that is well known for "their high concentration of intelligent and academic parents". A good response to this is to remind these parents and teachers that trash cans are full of college applications from straight "A" students who have been unable to write anything but a tepid and common entrance essay because they never got out and did anything beyond the ordinary after school activities. And can we ever pass up an opportunity to allow our children to discover the gift of empathy and the joy of connecting with someone different?

It has been my experience that aides are everywhere. Here is a great check list to determine if a student will be a good aide.

1. Is the student at least a few years older, both chronologically and emotionally, than the general population of your classroom?

2. Is this student willing to behave in a wacky and silly manner, without looking uncomfortable, annoyed or bored?

3. Does the student want to help?

4. Can the student be in class for almost every session?

5. Is the student willing to spend friendly social time with each student before and after class, and

acknowledge them in a friendly enthusiastic manner when they see them outside of class?

6. Is the student interested in having fun?

If you and the student can review these questions together and come up with the answer "yes" for each one, then you have found your aide. You may want to spend a session with your aides only, or have a 15 minute power meeting before each class to let them know what you are up to. Treat them like your colleagues, not your go-fers.

If you have female aides and male students, you may encounter budding crushes, usually on the part of your male students. Don't call attention to this in class, but don't let it slide either. Your aides should know that no romantic relationship should ever develop during the duration of class, and that even well meaning flirting or acceptance of attention could give the wrong impression. Then, explain to the student with the crush that the object of their affection is your employee, and that it would be inappropriate for there to be romance. Be clear, be blunt. Arrange your class so that there is space between the two kids and try not to pair them up together. This sort of thing happens in my class occasionally because a few of my aides are Jeanie's daughters and their friends. You have never seen a bevy of more beautiful young women. Gorgeous, every last one of them. Last year, we had a young man who was reticent to understand that his constant attention toward one of them was going nowhere. I finally got it across to him by saying, "It's like if you had a crush on me." That seemed to sufficiently appall him, and he kept his comments platonic after that.

Use your aides to stir the class up, to demonstrate hard to grasp concepts and to keep the class going. When you have a group of enthusiastic people on your side, somehow even the toughest things can seem worth doing.

First Day of Class

The first day of class is primarily you running the show. Most of the exercises you'll teach the kids are used to develop improvisational or thinking-on-your-feet skills, but for now, never put them in a situation where they have to come up with a specific answer. Remember, you are creating a fun, exclusive club. Somewhere they want to come back to.

The first thing I do while kids are showing up is work the crowd. I try to avoid that weird adult-bending-over "well-hi-little-fella-what's-you're-name?" type of thing. That used to really disturb me when I was a kid. A better approach is to sit down next to a kid. Just "be" for a minute or two. Don't look at 'em. Don't ignore 'em. They'll start checking you out. After awhile I usually say "Why are all these people here?" or "What's going on?" My first day of class, only one of my students had any idea it was an acting class. Three didn't know and one kid thought he might be getting an examination and a shot. Even after they found out it was an acting class, I was surprised to hear what they thought that might entail. Several students were convinced that they were going to have homework.

SHOTS AND HOMEWORK. NO WONDER EVERYONE LOOKED A LITTLE TENSE.

Here's my best suggestion for the first day. Never let them know that you're scared to death. And you may well be. I know I was. That has nothing to do with how terrific you'll be as an acting teacher. You are just walking into the great unknown and that's nerve-wracking. But, here's the cool thing. They are probably scared to death, too. Immediately, you can be on the same mental page with your students, a place where ordinary classroom teachers can never really be.

While we're on the subject, let's talk about the structure of this classroom as opposed to a more conventional classroom. I'm not just speaking of what the room looks like, but about your time structure, relationship with the students and classroom discipline. Obviously, the room will be different. No desks, chairs, chalkboards etc. It is best to have the students in a semi-circle of no more than four or five students in a row. Sitting on the carpet works best. You, however, should be sitting on a chair. Sitting on the floor in a small group gives the kids a feeling of security and you being in a higher spot gives them a good idea of where to focus. Plus, if a kid needs to get away from the situation for a moment, they don't have far to travel to feel as though they have left the group.

The relationship between you and your students must develop in a very particular way. You must be the silliest, craziest, most goofy, most outrageous person in that entire room. And your kids must love you. To be the silliest person in the room only requires that you are willing to be so. And your kids will love you as soon as they realize that you like them for who they truly are. I know that sounds very New Age, but it's not meant to. It's just true.

I tell my students that they don't need to worry about <u>looking</u> strange, because I am the biggest fool in the entire universe (at which point one of my students whose special interest is astronomy asks me to be more specific). No one will ever look as foolish as me, because I am a professional fool. This is not a dare; this is simply how it is. Kids don't worry about being silly, they worry about looking silly in front of others. If you show them you are willing to do something a little scary, like pretend to be an elephant with a head cold or that your tushy is made of Jello, then maybe they will try something a little scary like make eye contact, initiate a conversation, or smile.

After announcing yourself as a professional goof-ball, give them a rule to chew on. As I said, I really do run my class like a regular acting class, and the best acting teacher I ever had (thank you Steve McConnell) started my first acting class with this:

FIRST RULE OF ACTING! NEVER HURT AN ACTOR!

The class and I might then chat about how this means no hitting or weird touching. This also means no name calling and no unkind behavior. Since the class never hurts an actor, they must treat <u>themselves</u> carefully and kindly as well. You may find that a kid wants to take this opportunity to voice his woes about people who have treated him poorly. At this point, it is better to keep things moving along. Catch up with that kid during the social break and ask him for more details then.

By now, they should be acclimated to the fact that nothing painful or miserable will be happening to them. Now is the time to indoctrinate them into the secret world of Thesbianism. Oooooooh. Aaaaaaah.

You - REPEAT AFTER ME UNTIL I "SAY GORILLA"!

You - (in a silly voice) I PROMISE!

Students - (no doubt mumbling) I promise.

You - Hey, you guys, that's not the way I said it. Say it exactly the way I say it.

You - I PROMISE!

Students - (better) I Promise!

You - (changing your voice every line and pausing for students to repeat)

TO BE VERY, VERY SILLY.

SOOOOOOOOOOOOO SILLY,

SO VERY, VERY SILLY,

THAT I WILL NOT BE AFRAID

OF LOOKING SILLY IN FRONT OF …

(gasp) OTHER PEOPLE!

I WILL BE BRAVE ENOUGH

TO PRETEND TO BE

A YELLOW JELLY BEAN

STUCK IN SOMEONE ELSE'S NOSE!

I PROMISE

TO BE THAT SILLY

UNTIL SUCH DATE, TIME OR MOMENT AS MY
PARENT, GRANDPARENT OR GUARDIAN
REQUESTS ME TO CEASE, DESIST AND
OTHERWISE CURTAIL ALL STRANGE AND SILLY
BEHAVIOR.

GORILLA!!!!!

Most of the time the kids say "Gorilla" and you can say
"AAHH! You're not supposed to say anything after 'Gorilla.'"
Hee, hee, snort, snort, chuckle, chuckle.

You may have noticed by now that there is mention of tushies
and flatulent sounds and things up people's noses. Usually,
and for good reason, these topics are not nurtured as appropriate
conversation among the younger set. But in acting class, these
topics are worth their weight in gold. Nothing breaks down the
all-powerful-teacher-pathetic-worthless-student perception
quicker than watching that teacher pull imaginary Moray eels
out of her nostril. And, I read somewhere that a well-fabricated
sound of flatulence is the one thing that makes people laugh,
regardless of age, race, culture or education level. Frankly, I

can't afford to throw an opportunity like that away because it may be indelicate. Of course, too much of a good thing can get out of hand quickly, and I don't suggest that your acting class double as a show that would fit on a late night cable network. There is no denying, however, that a well-timed raspberry in the face of polite and petrified students moves mountains of stress away in the way that no verbal encouragement can. Plus, it reinforces the fact that in this secret club, certain privileges go along with working on such difficult and top secret material.

Most people worry that when they ask a group of kids a question that needs an enthusiastic response, they will instead be met with, the heart stopping evil- "Classroom By Rembrandt" or "The Blank Stare". My mother used to refer to it as "The Look." You know what I mean. There are a few ways to deal with this phenomenon.

1. Keep the pace fast and furious.

2. Don't ask the kids if they are ready to do something or if it sounds like fun. They will joyfully tell you, "No!" So don't ask.

3. Rely on your student aides (insert the words irreplaceable angels) to start and keep things moving. You can even prep them to respond in a way other than you require. You can gently steer them back on track, and your Asperger's students

can observe how you deal with Da, da, DAAAAH, Wrong Answers! The fear of all students! Oh, and by the way, this is how you deal with wrong answers:

"Oooo. Close."

"Hmm. I never thought of it that way."

"My what a vibrant and unique mind you have there."

4. Suggest outrageous things.

You - Why would someone have a happy face?

Students - The Look.

You - Could it be because Wolfgang here in the front row turned into a fuzzy purple watermelon and did the hoochie-cootchie dance?

5. Rely on your student aides to respond enough for everyone.

Your student aides, teachers helpers, or as I like to think of them, the most irreplaceable aspect of my class, will be your saving grace.

Getting to Know Each Other

Learning names can be a fun thing to do. Introduce yourself and then ask the class to say their names all together on the count of three so that you can learn them faster. Count off and fall off your seat when the wave of names hits you. Nope, you say, that isn't going to work. Have each kid say their name individually. Repeat their name. Really? Are they sure that's their name? Well, okay, if they say so. Each time a kid says their name, repeat the names of the children who have gone before them, until you are repeating the name of every student in a row. Make frequent mistakes. Try not to obviously blank on a kid's name, just insert a funny one instead. And, if a kid is too shy to say his name, just give him one. Here are a list of funny names. May I apologize for unintentionally offending anyone who has one of these names, express my seething jealousy that you have such an interesting handle and end by saying my own grandfather had the name at the top of the list.

- Herman

- Amaryllis

- Wolfgang

- Georgie-Porgie

- Sweetums

- Brunhilda

- Penelope

- Hermione

- Thor

- Ivan

- Rapunzel

- Katywumpus

- Sven

- Norman

- Mathilda

- Arthur

The kids love it when you make a mistake. And they love it even more when you remember their names. Sometimes they ask you to call them by a nickname. Make every effort to do so. Cool kids have nicknames. One little boy asked me to call him something different every class, from Patrick the Starfish to Master of the Universe. No problem. When I asked him why he didn't want me to use his real name, he said, "because it gets yelled at me all day long in school. And besides, you'll do anything."

After repeating their names and making mistakes, tell them you are going to close your eyes and they are to switch spaces in five seconds. Open your eyes and repeat their names one by one. It sounds simple, but I think some of my students would be happy and entertained if I did this for a whole class period.

Setting the Pace

So. Your first class and the ball is rolling. In the second section of this book, you will find descriptions of exercises we use in class. There is also a sort of lesson plan mapped out for each class to help you along. You'll be arranging things to fit your own class before you know it.

But don't worry, I'm not abandoning you quite yet. There are still a few things you may want to know.

A ratio of two or three crazy exercises to one relaxing exercise, in that order, keeps students happy. Usually. Some days my kids had so much energy they could have powered light bulbs, so I worked them hard. Other days, they were sad and depressed and spent most of the time counting imaginary clouds to soothing music. You'll know.

Have a student who won't participate? Don't make him. When was the last time you ever enjoyed something you were made to do? When a student won't participate, ask yourself:

1. Can I or one of my aides (insert the words inestimable treasures) easily see and monitor the student without stopping class?

2. Is the student safe?

3. Is the student responding in a kind way to the behaviors of others?

4. Is the class situated in a position so that the student could secretly participate or sneak into the group?

If the answer to these questions is "yes," leave the kid alone. If not, rectify the situation as quickly and cleanly as possible with no discussion and move forward with your class. That last question pertaining to the student's ability to secretly participate is important. Many times the act of joining a social group is far more appalling to a student than, say, picking pickles off an imaginary talking hamburger or speaking whale language like Dory in *Finding Nemo*. If students are allowed to sneak into a group, or quietly follow along from a safe distance, they may really enjoy themselves. When a student does start to participate, never stop class to praise her. "Oh, look kids, Brunhilda is part of the group now. Great way to successfully interact in a complex social matrix, kiddo. Rock on!"

EEK!

Rather, smile at her during the exercise, or when giving group praise, add her name. If that. I had a student who used to walk into every class with a scowl on his face, sit in a corner and loudly tell anyone passing by that he was not going to participate. Ever! Sometimes in some very colorful language. My aides (insert the words - those without whom I would perish) and I decided we would just accept that, say "Okay, that's cool." and leave it at that. Without fail, this student would then enthusiastically participate in every exercise. That is, until anyone commented on it. Then, scowling and grumbling back in the corner even after he had a great day, he'd leave saying how boring it had been and that he would never return. We always saw him next week. Maybe it was his way of controlling his environment. Who knows?

Occasionally, a student comes to class so terrified that he is truly unable to join in. This usually happens when class has met a few sessions and the student is new to the group. New students always seem to show up when the class is working on something particularly bizarre. They could pop in when we are stretching or deep breathing, but oh no, they always seem to appear while we are slogging through imaginary chocolate pudding with giant imaginary marshmallows strapped to our feet. Great first impression. When this happens, I ask one of my aides (insert the word gems) to monitor and continue the exercise. I calmly walk over to the kid, making no eye contact. Once, a new student saw me approach, lost all color and mouthed "No, no, no." Okay, no problem. I just sat down next to him. We watched the class together. "I am so glad you're here," I said. He just looked at me. "I am really nervous," I said, "because there are so many people here today and I'm scared I won't be a good teacher. Could you stay here and peek around the door once in a while and make sure everyone is being nice to me? Thanks! Phew! I feel better now that I know you're here." Always try to give the scared student some way to participate, even if it's "Could you make sure that I don't start sprouting giant mushrooms out of my ears? Just let me know if that starts to happen. Thanks."

Eventually this boy walked around the classroom with me while the other students worked independently in smaller groups. He later told me he thought he was going to have to stand in front of everyone, say his name, and answer questions. "What kind of questions?" I asked. Ones, he said, he didn't know the answers to.

Don't be fooled by the kid self-stimming in the corner. Chances are, he's watching every move you make. Often times, I start every class with the same two or three exercises, to orient the kids and give them a sense of repetition and safety. One day, a student who had spent every class humming and spinning in the corner, calmly approached me. I was then given a list of errors that I had made in my opening routine. Then, back he went to the corner. Every single one of his observations was dead on.

A few words about self-stimming (rocking, flapping, humming, etc.). As long as it isn't too distracting or in any way dangerous, let your students do it. I have a student who is very flexible and tends to nibble his toes. Not a behavior you would want to see in English Class, perhaps, but in the elite realm of acting class, this can either be easily ignored, or looked upon with admiration. Another student tends to softly collapse and remain still on the floor for several seconds. During this time, we just keep going, speaking to him and responding for him in funny voices. He gets back up as if nothing had happened. The only time he gets stubborn about it is if we try to make him get up.

Sometimes parents come to watch, and they get stressed when they see their child rock or flap or whatever. They may try to control or refocus the child as a way of helping you. Assure those parents that their child's behavior is okay in the class. Many parents have told me that their children frequently get thrown out of groups. Many students tell me acting class is the only place where they can just be themselves. I like to see kids who recognize that they are getting stressed and then do something to try to relieve that stress. Maybe they aren't consciously making that choice, but on some level they are saying, "I need a break so I can remain with this group."

Far more likely than an unresponsive or preoccupied student, is the student who wants to run your class. They want to participate too much. Occasionally, these are the kids who have been in a play and who walk in expecting to be fitted for a costume, handed a script and put out on stage. These are the kids who, after a few sessions will say in a disgusted tone, "When are we going to start the ACTING class?!" Or you will have a student who wants to add on to your every comment, point out errors in syntax or content or who will steal focus just at the moment you were getting to your point by making a large farm animal noise. The best way to deal with these students is to let them have their say (abbreviated by an enthusiastic "GOOD!") and to be brief and honest with them. When they keep going or, in some cases, state clearly that they were not done speaking, let them know that you are interested, but that the class needs to keep moving forward. And then, <u>move forward</u>. Always, always take some time after class or at break to follow up with these students, referring specifically to what they were talking about. Let them talk to you.

Once I made the mistake of telling an overly talkative student that I needed him to be my assistant to help me improve the class. Whoa, Nelly!

Never in my life had I had such a dedicated and driven assistant. Until we restructured the parameters of his job, I barely made it out of the building with my ego intact. Later, we decided that he would keep his reports to five minutes after class, he wouldn't tattle on anyone, and he would try to spare my feelings. Now, I couldn't do without him.

Some kids won't like your class. Currently, we live in an age where "no child is left behind." Sometimes, however, a student is simply not suited to acting class. This is not leaving a child behind. This is honoring the child as an individual. It is cruel and useless to subject a child to an experience that, for whatever reason, makes him consistently miserable, no matter how good it's supposed to be for him. If it is apparent that, after a few sessions, the child is acting out and obviously unhappy, let the kid off the hook and suggest he do some other type of social skills work. Students who quit my class were very clear on why. They didn't like acting. They knew it, I knew it, and we parted on friendly terms.

Why Acting Helps

Hopefully by now I have convinced you that running an acting class is absolutely within your grasp. So now let's talk about why we really teach them acting. We teach them acting so that they can develop and master key social skills that will allow them to successfully interact with friends and co-workers for the rest of their lives. Acting class does this in two ways. First, the exercises themselves teach the kids the nuts and bolts about things neurotypical folks intrinsically understand. The ability to read body language, react appropriately to it and use it to express feelings are key tools for any actor. It is also a key deficit in students with Asperger's Syndrome. Modulation of voice in order to convey an emotion is essential to any good performance as well as coming in handy in ordinary conversation. Almost as important is the time your students will spend in class just bonding while tackling a challenging task, or encouraging a shy student to perform. We frequently have a bit of before and after time tacked on to each session. It is there that I see the students generalize the skills they have learned in that day's lesson. Many times parents tell us that their child will start encouraging them to get the car ready hours and hours before class starts to make sure that they arrive on time. I know it is not only me they want to see, but their acting buddies with whom they share a communal experience. You have an amazing opportunity here. Not only can you show them how talented they are, but give them the chance to learn the building blocks with which they will build their life-long relationships.

The exercises in this book are broken down into several sections. They start simple, requiring very little from the student. Each exercise builds upon the one that came before. Your students will start out working in a group on highly structured tasks. As they continue through the sessions, they will start to work in smaller, more independent groups, on tasks that require more input and creativity from them. On a similar note, you will notice that students will spend several classes using only their body. Later, they will add sound and gibberish noise to the exercises, eventually progressing to short scripted lines. Eventually, many acting students progress to being able to create their own text in an improvisational way. No matter how advanced your students seem in the beginning, do not skip steps. Oh, they'll want to. In this way, they are no different than neurotypical actors. Always looking for a great costume and a spotlight. But like any young actor, they have to build their talent from the ground up. First the body, then the words. It ain't glamorous, but it works.

By now, you practical types are tapping your feet thinking, "When are we going to get to the nuts and bolts of this operation?" And you're absolutely right.

Practical Stuff

Plan to start your class either during the summer, one to two months after school begins or in late January, early February. If you start your class when school starts, parents will have a hard time scheduling you in and kids will be sleepy and stressed. Plus, you are probably either a parent or someone who works with children, so the start of school is a busy time for you, too!

First, find a space. Organize your thoughts and be clear on what you can compromise upon and what you cannot. You may be able to work in a space that needs the furniture in it moved before each class but you cannot work in a space with no available bathrooms. When scouting out places, bring this statement of purpose and list of requirements with you. Many places are willing to donate space for a good cause. Here's a sample.

Mission Statement

To provide an opportunity for students with High Functioning Autism and Asperger's Syndrome to learn and practice basic social skills through the study of beginning acting techniques in a safe, supportive and fun environment tailored to their specific needs. Students will explore their unique ability to perform theatrically while becoming more comfortable with essential life skills.

The Class

Students will study techniques such as improvisation, tableau, mime, self scripting and the development of humor. Class will focus on reading contextual clues, body language and theory of mind. Understanding and responding to non-verbal clues such as facial expression and tone of voice will be studied as well as understanding and expressing emotions. The class will culminate in a short performance of skills studied for an audience of family and friends.

Time Requirement

Wednesdays, 4:00-5:00 pm, from June 12-August 15

Teacher

This is YOU! Include your experience, education and things you may be known for locally, such as previous work with children.

Requirements

- 5-8 students with Asperger's Syndrome or High Functioning Autism

- 4-5 neurotypical peers

- 1-2 adults to monitor free time and participate in games

- Large, open room

- Quiet and private

- No mirrors visible to students

- Carpeted floor

- Central heating and cooling

- Easy, close access to bathrooms

- Situated so that noise from students will not be disturbing to others

- Permission for students to eat a small neat snack

- Minimal fee or free of charge

- Students must be dropped off and picked up in a timely manner, as there will be no supervision available before or after class.

- Parents may be required to sign a liability waiver to satisfy the needs of the location provider.

Once you have secured a space, you may need to advertise. A class with less than five students is very hard to keep going. Use whatever it takes to get the word out. I hear the "web" is pretty popular. I am computer-deficient to the point that I would have had this book printed in my own handwriting if I could have gotten away with it. Luckily, I have Dr. Jeanie McAfee (insert words: World Famous Author of *Navigating the Social World*, Brilliant Woman, Partner, Dear and Patient

Friend) in my corner to help me with things like this. She has been kind enough to organize an advertisement on her web site, refer students to acting class, bring goodies and basically do all the organizational work while I flit around class like a social butterfly with an extra wing. I highly recommend that you find a partner to help you with the execution of this type of project. The stability of having someone in on everything you are planning to do is invaluable. Jeanie also films sections of the class for later reference.

When you advertise your class, please don't use the dry description that you carry with you when looking for a location. The bottom line is that the class is fun, fun, FUN!

Here is a description very similar to the one Jeanie posted for our first acting class.

Calling all actors! Announcing a dynamic and fast-paced acting program that focuses on the development of social skills through the use of wild and wacky theater games. Dynamic classes for youth ages 6-19 address social cognition, pragmatic language and teamwork. Improvisation and comedy will highlight each student's unique abilities and provide an exciting and silly atmosphere for students to learn key social skills such as reading non-verbal cues, sequencing, perspective taking and theory of mind. Friends and family will join us for a final performance, and may be asked to join in the fun!

Feel free to include students with other developmental needs on a case to case basis. In general, if the student is verbal, responsive and capable of functioning in a group environment, give it a try. I have a student who is a bit lower functioning than the rest of the group, but her father takes class with her, helping her along as we progress through the exercises. It is great to see the pair work every week, as well as to see the rest of the class nurture her and encourage her to participate. Currently, our class contains a wide range of learning disabilities and behavioral issues, including myself who is wildly dyslexic. We all seem to find a way to make it work. As I have said before, kids will do fun stuff if they possibly can, regardless of what their diagnosis allows.

After you have secured enough students for your class, it is a great idea to send a letter to parents. Here is a sample.

Dear Parents/Guardians,

Hooray! We are delighted that your child will be joining us for our upcoming acting sessions. We are excited to meet _____, and hope to have the pleasure of your company as well. You are invited to participate in class at any time.

We have sent along information about the time and location of class, as well as a list of things your student will need to make the class a terrific experience.

Class begins on ____, ____,____. Class will take place every _____, from _____ to _____. There will be no supervision before or after class, so please make arrangements to drop off and pick up your child in a timely manner. Please come into the class to pick up your child. Your child's consistent attendance is not required, but please understand that the extent of your child's participation in the final event may be determined by how many classes he has attended. The more _____ comes to class, the more comfortable he will be and the more fun he will have.

Classes will be held at _____

(Insert address and directions as necessary)

Your child will need:

Comfortable loose clothing (girls should wear pants)

A pair of close fitting, rubber soled slippers (no bunny ears, please)

A neat, healthful, and easy to eat snack and a clear beverage.

Our class will run _____ weeks. Our final class will run a bit longer than usual, as we will be giving a performance on that day.

Again, we are looking forward to working with _____. Please call us with any questions or concerns you may have.

Thanks!

A week before your class begins, pop by the site and hang out in the room during the time that your class will take place. Observe any strange noises, smells or people that may invade your area. This way, you can head off problems before they arise, and have an answer every time one of your students asks, "What was that?"

On the day before your class begins, touch base with everyone involved with your space. Double check that the space will be available, the lights will be on and the temperature will be livable. Make sure the bathrooms will be open. Remind them that you're coming and that you're going to be LOUD. I say this because the group of students you will be working with are not known for their ability to "go with the flow." You want to be absolutely confident that you have taken care of everything you have control over. That way, when the unexpected happens, you won't have to worry that someone may turn the lights out halfway through class and lock you in, too. While we are on the subject of LOUD, remember this: Many of our kids have auditory sensitivities, so you need to play your class's volume level by, (ha, ha), ear. Try to find a happy medium that all students can work with.

Well, you're all set. Now all you have to do is take a look at the exercises in the second section. Try them out with family and friends. Get them under your belt. I envy you your first acting class because you are going to have so much fun. Even on days when everything seems to be falling apart, you'll always have those one or two students who make your day. Just last week, five minutes before class, as I battled the flu and tried to quickly schedule the plumber to come fix our pipes while simultaneously searching for my missing car keys and blowing my nose, one of my students ran up and said, "Hey Amelia, cheer up! I brought my happy face to class for you!" Soon, you will have stories like that to tell.

Part 2

The Exercises

Each section of exercises is important to the development of the actor. It is not necessary to do all of the variations to each exercise, but it is important that you follow the order of the exercises. Don't race through them. Each class is different, and you don't need to get through everything in this book in order to have a challenging and exciting class. When an exercise requires students to form pairs or groups, you should assign where people go. It will save time and allow you to curtail any behavior problems before they arise.

Working the Body

These exercises work the large muscle groups, encourage group dynamics and coordination. Most encourage the class to work together and to tolerate one another.

1. Mirror Exercises

When performing any of these exercises, be sure to follow the following procedure.

1. Start big and slow.

2. Make sure your partner can follow you at all times.

3. Keep constant eye contact instead of looking at the part that is moving.

Group Mirror:

Face the group. Tell the group that you need them to be your mirror. They will have to do anything you do. Remind them that if you move your left side, they will move their right side, because they are mirroring you. Remind them that since they are a mirror, they should make no noise. Start out with slow, simple movements that isolate one body part at a time. Work up to moving several body parts simultaneously. For students who find it painful to make eye contact, have them focus on the leaders face. The point is not to break concentration during the exercise by looking at each body part as it moves.

Variations:

- Perform the group mirror using your face only.

- Perform the group mirror with the class in a circle. Explain to the students that they should not worry about being able to see the person leading the mirror exercise, but should focus on the person directly in front of them. If everyone does this, the correct movement will be telegraphed around the entire circle.

- Have students pair up and perform the mirror together. Have them switch leadership back and forth between them during the exercise.

- Have the students form a circle, and ask one student to leave. While that student is out of the room, decide who the leader of the mirror exercise will be and have them begin a simple, repetitive movement. Allow the student outside to reenter. Have the guessing student join the group, and try to determine who is leading. Periodically, the hidden leader should change the movement. The trick is for the students to focus on those directly in front of them and not telegraph who is leading by staring at them.

2. Amoebae

Students gather in a tight group. Have them close their eyes. Ask them to follow the sound of your voice while moving as a group. They may not like this one right away, but there's nothing better at creating a group dynamic. Start slowly, and encourage the group to move without crushing anyone, nor leaving anyone behind. Be vigilant against peekers. In the beginning, keep a constant monologue for the group to orient on. As you see them become more comfortable, sneak around and surprise them with your voice from different places in the room.

3. Fishies

Students form a line with you as the leader. They must walk as closely behind one another as possible. Lead them at a brisk pace around the room, abruptly stopping unexpectedly. The goal of the group is to keep pace with you and for everyone to stop immediately and at once, with no bumps.

Variations:

Switch styles of movement as they follow you.

Have the group move in a clump or "school." Stragglers get caught up by the tickle shark or some such thing. Tailor your consequences to what the caught child can tolerate. Getting caught should have a silly and delightful consequence, not one that will stress the kid out. Being tickled isn't fun for all of us. Air tickling seems to work well.

4. Samurai

This is an exercise I learned while working for The Missoula Children's Theater. This is an excellent company that tours the country and produces plays with community children as the stars. They are committed to giving every child a wonderful experience in the theater. I cannot recommend them highly enough!

Have students form lines of two or three, one behind the other, leaving ample room between each student. You are the samurai. Using large movements accompanied by a bloodcurdling yell, make a large cutting movement in a certain direction of the group. Students respond accordingly.

You cut right, they jump left.

You cut left, they jump right.

You cut front, they jump back.

You cut under their feet, they jump up. (I usually tell my kids that they can't come out of the air until I say so, chuckle-chuckle, snort-snort)

You cut over the top of their heads, they crouch on the floor. They are not allowed to stand up until you bow at them.

When you play the game, mix up the order of your movements so that you take the class by surprise.

Again, start slowly and be forgiving of late jumpers and those who are directionally impaired. But only for a while. The kids don't like it if you cut them too much slack once they get good at this game.

Variations:

Eventually, the kids will want to take turns being the samurai. Remind them that they must be clear and big with their movements, and come up with some noise to accompany each cut.

5. Pencil Tush

Have the students stand up, leaving at least a two-person space between each of them.

Have them imagine that there is a huge pencil TAPED to their tushies, with the writing end pointing down. It is very important to stress the word taped, lest you get colorful remarks.

Tell them they are standing on the world's largest piece of paper.

They are to think of the one thing that drives them crazy, really makes them mad.

Now, the students write the name of this person or thing in big letters with their pencil. I remind them to dot their "i"s and cross their "t"s.

They then think of the one thing that makes them the happiest.

Have them re-tape the pencil to one of their elbows.

Students must write the name of the thing that makes them happy.

Then, have students switch elbows and write the happy thing backwards.

6. Going for a Walk

Have the students meander around the room. They may not walk together in a straight line or walk away and stay away from the group. They must take a walk by themselves but still be part of the group in some way. This gets pretty boring quickly, so get going on those variations as soon as possible.

Variations:

Have the group imagine that they are walking through different materials in different quantities. Encourage the students to really think about each material and what it would feel like, what problems they might have while walking through it. Here is a list of some interesting materials

- Chocolate pudding

- Sand

- Cotton balls

- Wet leaves

- Snot - Yes, I know. This is not a very nice word, but is mucus any better?

- Chicken feathers

- Marshmallow fluff

- Ping-pong balls

- Dirty socks

- Mini trampolines

Encourage them to imagine the differences between slogging through ankle-high Marshmallow Fluff and chest-high Marshmallow Fluff. It is extremely important that they do not stop and think about these changes, but simply make them as they keep moving. The group should be moving constantly. You may notice students forming allies to help each other move through space, which is perfectly acceptable.

Use Music

Once the group is familiar with this exercise, have them move to music, drastically changing the music every 30 to 60 seconds. I have rather eclectic musical tastes, so I bring everything from Etta James to Verdi to Chants of the Tibetan Monks. I also include ambient noise, like ocean waves and city noises. Once I saw an entire group of self-conscious kids turn into a swamp of creatures when I played sounds from a Louisiana Bayou. I suggest you make a special tape with about 6 to 10 minutes of sound samples on it to save you the trouble of hopping up and down to change the music. Besides, if I haven't mentioned it before, you will be doing all these things with your students. There is something magical about dancing with your kids as you watch them physically relax right in front of you.

7. Different Centers of the Body

Students walk around the room imagining that there is a string attached to a certain part of their body and it is pulling them forward (you decide). Call out different body parts as they walk. Students are allowed to walk awkwardly for awhile, but encourage your students to imagine that this is the way they walk all the time. Tell them to try to find a way to make it work. Some good body parts are:

- Head

- Belly

- Nose

- Chin

- Tushy

- Kneecaps

As students walk, ask them to think about how a character walking this way would feel. They don't need to come up with logical reasons why a person would walk this way, just what kind of personality a character might have. Tell them this is a first step towards character development in acting.

8. Laban

Laban is a way of describing movement created by Rudolf Laban. In his *Mastery of Movement*, Laban breaks down physical movement into eight different categories. He organizes the types of movement like this:

Strong Weight Movement

- Puncher-(direct and quick)

- Presser-(direct and sustained)

- Slasher-(flexible and quick)

- Wringer-(flexible and sustained)

Light Weight Movement

- Dabber-(direct and quick)

- Glider-(direct and sustained)

- Flicker-(flexible and quick)

- Floater-(flexible and sustained)

When introducing your students to the concept of Laban, don't explain the details. Just have them start moving around the room. Tell them you are going to say a word, and you want them to reflect that word with the way they are moving through space. Tell them to use their whole body, altering the speed, intensity, and focus of their gait based on the word you say. Go through all eight words; punch, press, slash, wring, dab, glide, flick, and float. Students move to each word for a few minutes. Then …

Ask them to choose the one they felt most comfortable with and progress through the room, using this type of movement.

Then, tell them to switch to the one they had most difficulty with.

Variations:

Form students into pairs. Give each student a contrasting Laban movement quality. Have students converse with only body movements. Some good parings are:

- Punch and Float

- Flick and Slash

- Dab and Press

- Wring and Glide

Advanced students can explore how Laban movement can affect speech patterns and tone of voice. This is an excellent way to create a character, and should be referred to when students start creating their own skits.

9. Dance Steps

It's never a bad idea to teach the group how to "cut a rug." The very act of telling them that you will be teaching them how to "cut a rug" will require some explaining, since your students probably won't be adept at idioms. This is a great opportunity to prep one of your aides to pull out a big pair of scissors and declare "I'm READY!"

Simple steps such as the box step, waltz, fox-trot or cha-cha can be transformed into great performances when accompanied by the right music and the proper introduction. This is a good time to split the group in two and have them perform for one another. Props like fans, scarves and hats can add to the show. Encourage each subgroup to perform the step several times, then improvise for several bars, finishing up with a group execution of the step.

10. Machines

When teaching any machine exercise, emphasize that the group's goal is to create a machine that not only has individual parts, but obviously works as a whole towards some common task.

Simple Machine:

One student starts off with a simple, easily repeatable movement. It's a good idea to have your aides be the first few participants in this exercise, because they can model good choices and they will also be repeating their movement for a long time. Each student hops into the machine, linking on to one pre-existing part and adding their own movement. Initially, you will see a group of kids standing in front of you, doing their own thing without connecting to each other. Once, when this was occurring, someone accidentally walked into class, then quickly ran away. I wonder what he thought I was doing to them. Guide your students to interact with each other by picking up on each other's rhythm. Have them ask themselves, "Where can I fit in?" Eventually, your students will create great big heaps of movement, all linked to one another.

Variations:

Hot and Cold Machine

One student leaves the room. The rest of the group decide on an object in the room. The group sits in a tight clump in a section of the room with a clear vantage point of the object. Tell them not to stare directly at the object, only at the student who comes back into the room. This student must locate the object based on the intensity of noise that comes from the group or "Hot and Cold Machine." The closer the student gets to the object, the more intense the noise gets. Finally, when the student places his hand on the object, the group yells, "Great Googly Moogly!" For classes that have students hypersensitive to sound, the machine can recite letters of the alphabet instead, "A" for coldest and "Z" for hottest.

Other Machines

Have students create small machines for a peer audience. Have students comment on which machines are really interesting and connected and why.

Have students gather in small groups. Give each group a card with the type of machine they are to create. Start with simple, recognizable machines:

- Washing machine

- Train

- Pie maker

- Pencil sharpener

and progress on to stranger things ...

- Ear wax collector

- Butterfly wing maker

- Ice cream sundae eater

Have each group construct the machine for their peer audience and have the watching students guess what it might be. They may rarely guess correctly, but this is a great opportunity to let them in on a little secret about art. As long as YOU know what you're doing, the art will be good. It doesn't matter if your audience can tell exactly what you're up to as long as it's good. Good art encourages people to imagine things and "fill in the blanks." I tell them, as artists, it is your job to inspire the masses to imagine as much as possible. So, if your audience doesn't guess what you're doing even after a few hints, just smile and tell them they are right. After swearing them to secrecy, I let them in on another little secret. Audiences, I tell them, are not very bright. They don't see things as clearly as we actors do. It is our job to keep the audience feeling confident and smart so that they will continue to keep imagining and some sweet day be as creative as we are.

11. Dolls

This is an exercise that teaches skills used in many other exercises. The key to "dolls" is to have the student being the doll freeze and remain still for the duration of the exercise. This is rather difficult and requires a lot of muscle control. You can help your students develop this skill by giving them the following hints.

1. Always make sure your knees are slightly bent and your tushy is relaxed. Otherwise, your brain won't get any blood to it and you'll pass out or throw up or something equally as inconvenient.

2. Make sure you have your weight distributed evenly over both feet. No one can balance forever.

Pair up with your student aide. Explain that this aide is now a doll. You will be molding your doll to express a single emotion, which the group is to identify. Explain that this is an irreplaceable doll and so you will therefore be treating it with the utmost delicacy and care. This might be a good time to review the first rule of acting with your class. Gently mold your doll to express a broad emotion, such as "happy." As you guide your doll into the correct positions, explain what you are doing and what the doll should do.

Example:

You: I am taking Eri's arm and I'm stretching it over her head to point up to the sky and she's going to hold it up there even after I let go. Now I'm going to tip back her chin so that she's looking up.

It's very important to let your doll know exactly what you are up to. This is an especially good habit to get into in case you work with a student who can't tolerate touch. I then do the "air touch," or decide to maneuver my doll with imaginary strings.

After you pose your doll, ask the peer audience to guess what emotion your doll is feeling. Tell them to explain to you exactly what led them to that decision. It is important to make them be very specific about what they see. Ask them about individual parts of the doll's body and what each part is doing

These are some basic emotions to start with:

- Happy

- Sad

- Angry

- Tired

- Sick

- Frightened

Here are some more subtle emotions to use when your class has mastered the broader ones:

- In love

- Puzzled

- Worried

- Confident

- Sneaky

Variations:

Have students get into groups or pairs. Give them cards with a list of similar emotions on it. Each student will choose one emotion and the group will present themselves as statues to the peer audience. Tell the audience which emotions are being portrayed and have them guess who is which. Encourage the students to point out similarities between each statue, and which differences give the answers away.

Some good grouping of emotions are:

- Tired and bored

- Sad and embarrassed

- Happy and confident

- In love and silly

- Lonely and worried

12. Snapshots

Here we take dolls to the next level by telling little stories with them. Students get into small groups and are given cards that have an event on them. The group must portray the event and its outcome in three doll pictures or "snapshots." The peer audience will hide their eyes while the group hits their first pose. The audience looks, makes assumptions and comments, them hides their eyes again while the group hits their second pose, and so on. Frequently, I ask the performing group to do it again from the top, so that the audience can really take a look at what is going on. Not all the students in the group must be in each snapshot, but I encourage them to think creatively, perhaps by portraying some essential inanimate object. These are events that are easy for students to grasp:

- A seed becomes a flower.

- A group of people win the lottery.

- A group of people discover a lit firecracker.

- Several people stranded on a deserted island see a boat.

- Someone eats the last cookie in the box.

You can make up whatever you want. Explain to the students that in order to tell a story in just three pictures, they must be clear on the most important elements of that story. They should also plan on adopting the before-during-after format. Have them portray what things are like before the event, how things are during the event and how things are after the event has occurred. Tell students that if they are portraying inanimate objects, they will be most effective if their face is not visible to the audience.

Here is an example:

SOMEONE EATS THE LAST COOKIE IN THE BOX!!!

1. Students A, B, and C sit in a line. Each student is portraying a different stage of happy eating. Student B seems to hold a box.

2. Students A, B, and C are looking in the box for another cookie and see that the box is empty. Each student is reacting differently. Student A is sobbing, Student C looks puzzled and Student B looks guilty.

3. Students A and C glare angrily at Student B while pointing at the box. Student B looks sheepish and helpless.

Or perhaps Students A and C pound Student B into jelly. Or Student B taunts Students A and C. Or furtively snarfs the cookie right under their noses. It doesn't matter how they interpret the situation's outcome, as long as they have clearly told the story.

Variation:

Students will come up with their own snapshots topics. This is a great way to deal with problems that may have happened to students during the day. It allows the experience to become a group experience, one that the students can slow down, examine and replay to their satisfaction. It gives them power over the problem and gives them the opportunity to rewrite the ending. That is the best thing about snapshots and tableau. By freezing the moment, the student is allowed to examine all the nuances of that moment at his own pace. So many times these kids are forced to go at someone else's pace. It's nice to give them a break.

13. Tableau

For the longest time, I thought the word tableau meant "picture" in French. While Jeanie and I were speaking at a conference in Grand Forks ND, a Canadian lady informed me that it actually means chalkboard. How cool! In any case, the idea is the same. A group of students tell a well-known story in five elaborate snapshots. For this exercise I find fairy tales work very well. The ones that lend themselves the best to this format are:

- *Cinderella*

- *Jack and the Bean Stalk*

- *Little Red Riding Hood*

- *Goldie Locks and the Three Bears*

- *Hansel and Gretel*

Snow White and the Seven Dwarfs gets very confusing and *Sleeping Beauty* has a mandatory kiss, which can get difficult if you only have male students.

As with Snapshots, the goal of each group should be to identify the key elements in their tale and find the clearest and most concise way to portray them. Spend a few class periods working on these, allowing time for each group to make choices, receive input from the group and rework their pieces.

Variations:

Have groups portray real life situations as tableau. Performing groups will leave off the final pose, and let the audience vote on what should happen. The performing group then portrays the audience choice.

Give a group a card with one word on it. Have them create a three-part tableau based on that word. Have the audience guess what the word is. Start with concrete words:

- Apple

- Puppy

- Homework

- Soda pop

- Pillow

and move on to more abstract words:

- Help

- City

- Parents

- Thanksgiving

- Sports

14. Passing Energy

Now we introduce sound to the body. Have the students form a circle. With you starting, make a small movement accompanied by a gibberish sound at the student directly next to you. This student will then turn and repeat that same sound and movement to the person next to them, and so on. It is vital that the student accept the noise and movement and then immediately send it on without pause or comment. When your own movement reaches you, change the movement.

Variations:

Have each student vary the sound and movement as they pass it on to the next person.

Instead of a noise, use a single word and an accompanying movement. Start as you did in the beginning, having the group repeat your word. When students have become comfortable with that, have each come up with their own word as they pass the energy along.

15. Gibberish

Students will now take another step closer to performing skits. Using gibberish as text is a wonderful way to key the student into what is important in any scene—the meaning behind what is being said. This is also a great way to teach the importance of inflection and tone of voice in communication. It's a lot of fun, too.

PB&J

Your gibberish should always be simple and fun to say. Having the students memorize difficult words like grethanbolopmethmuth may entertain you, but it won't do much for the class. Here are some good gibberish words:

- Snork

- Bleep

- Whoop

- Neener

- Diddly

- Fitsle

- Rammalama

- Zap

Although advanced students may want to try to use a combination of these sounds during scenes, and even come up with some of their own words, the best starting place is to assign a single word to the class and tell them that this is the only word in their language. Years ago, this might have been a difficult concept to accept. Now, however, we have Pokemon, where a character can only say it's name, regardless of what it's trying to express. Most kids are familiar with these characters and it's a great way to explain the use of gibberish in class.

Tell each student that he or she will be explaining the way to make a peanut butter and jelly sandwich. They may only use the one word of gibberish given to the class, but they may use it as many times as necessary. Tell them to go through each step needed to make a PB&J, as if we, the audience was very young. Encourage them to use their bodies as they explain the process.

If they seem stuck, having trouble understanding what to do, break the exercise down into little pieces and teach them the way to use gibberish. Explain to them that they need to say the gibberish the exact same way as if they were saying a real sentence. Like this-

"First, you get two pieces of bread."

Have the class say the sentence.

Ask the class- "Which words did we emphasize?" (usually the words "first" and "two" get the most emphasis)

Have the class exaggerate their inflection on those two words while they say the sentence again.

Ask the class- "What body movements could we use to help people understand what we are talking about?" (usually, holding up two fingers for the word two and holding hands out for bread works well)

Have the class say the sentence and do the movements.

Have the class use the same inflection and movements but use the gibberish word instead of the words in the sentence.

Variations:

Assign each student a different action to explain

Examples:

- How to cross the street

- How to wash your hair

- How to fly a kite

- How to paint toenails

- How to pet a puppy

- How to sneak up and scare someone

- How to shake hands

Notice that each action is simple and physical. Don't tell kids to explain how to get good grades in school or how to bring about world peace. Have each student keep their action a secret and make the class guess what they are talking about.

Yadda, Yadda, Yadda. Blah, Blah, Blah.

Teach the class this phrase: Yadda, yadda, yadda. Blah, blah, blah.

Have the class break up into pairs.

Give each pair a card with a clearly defined situation on it, as well as a predetermined outcome. (I'll give you examples at the end of the exercises description.)

Have each pair decide who will be "A" and who will be "B".

Have the "A"s practice saying Yadda, yadda, yadda.

Have the "B"s practice saying Blah, blah, blah.

Tell the class that this is the only script they get. They have to say the script exactly this way, with no omissions or additions. Actors can't help but try to add their own personal touches to a script. A talented young man in my class portraying a frustrated customer insisted on saying "Yadda, yadda, yadda, and I'm not kidding, buddy." Wonderful, I said, but all your emotion went into "… and I'm not kidding, buddy." I want you to put all that emotion into the words "Yadda, yadda, yadda." Pretend that you are saying "I'm not kidding, buddy" when your mouth is saying "Yadda, yadda, yadda. We'll come back to you in a few minutes." His performance the next time was much more expressive because he was showing us with his tone and body what he was trying to say.

Here are some easy scenes to start with:

- "A" is a robber telling "B" to hand over her diamond necklace. "B" screams for the police.

- "A" is a toddler trying to play with "B," a toddler who won't share his blocks.

- "A" is a person with scandalous gossip, and tells it to "B." "B" is shocked.

- "A" is a smitten lover asking "B" to go out on a date. "B" says yes.

- "A" is a customer in a restaurant and "B" is a busy waiter. "B" is frazzled.

- "A" is a child trying to get out of eating a steamed clam and "B" is her mother.

You may notice that in all of these scenarios, each character wants something. Tell your students that the more their character wants something, the better the scene will be. Here's an example.

"A" is trying to get out of eating a steamed clam. If the actor playing "A" decides that her character will say "Yadda, yadda, yadda" as if she were saying" I guess I won't eat this last clam," and "B" says "Blah, blah, blah" as if she were saying " I think you should, but it's all the same to me," it would be a pretty forgettable scene.

A better way to do it is make the stakes as high as possible. Have the pair imagine that their characters are in dire straights and must get each of their ways at all costs. Now, "A" will imagine that she has finally decided to become a vegetarian and here at the dinner table is where she will make her first move toward an exciting new life. She will never eat that clam, even if she has to sit there at that table until she is old and grey, even if the rest of the family gets to go out for ice cream while she sits at the table. No clam, no way. "A" now says "Yadda. yadda, yadda" as if she was saying " I will die before I eat that living booger in a shell."

The more important, the better. Maybe "A" is convinced that the clam is still alive. Or perhaps it has been laced with poison by secret agents.

"B," the Mom, instead of being indifferent to "A"s disobedience, should have an equally strong reaction. Perhaps they are both at a fancy restaurant at "A"s whining request, and the clam cost 17,000 dollars. Oh, and "B"s new boss is sitting at the next table. "B," says "Blah, blah, blah" as if she is saying "You'll eat that clam and you'll like that clam and you'll smile when you do it or you'll get a time out that'll take you through your college years. Now EAT THAT CLAM."

Your students will start to realize that the more intensity they put into anything they say, the more interesting it will be for the audience.

Variations:

A- Yadda.

B- yadda.

A- yadda.

B- Blah.

A- blah.

B- blah.

You can also add one or two more players to a group and have a more complex scene. The only requirements for a scenario are that each character has a clear desire that in some way involves the other character.

Group Storytelling

When we start getting into verbal improvisation, I let my kids know about a little creature inside their heads. Keith Johnstone, in his wonderful book *IMPRO,* describes a "watcher at the gates of the mind." An editor. Ordinarily, this editor is a great guy. He keeps us out of trouble at school, checks to make sure we are saying nice things, keeps us from tearing all our clothes off and running around naked. But here in acting class, we need to give our editor a vacation. He's worked hard all week long, so send him to Hawaii for an hour. This does not mean that we are going to say awful things and run around naked. It does mean, however, that we do not have to impress our editor. We are not going to <u>try</u> to be clever. We are not going to <u>try</u> to be funny. We are not going to <u>try</u> to be original. Again, Keith Johnstone (the great Keith Johnstone, go get his book) gives me a terrific example. A person trying to be original is like a person at the North Pole trying to go North. The harder they try, the farther away they end up from their goal. I ask the kids to think of a time when they were asked a simple question and they froze, being unable to think of anything to say. That, I tell them, is not because you didn't have anything to say, but because you had hundreds of ideas to say and they all got really excited and ran for the exit, your mouth. Your editor stopped them on the way and had to check each and every one. That took a lot of time. There you stood, saying nothing. Not because you had nothing to say, but because your editor was being a little too good at his job. That's why he needs to go eat pineapples on the beach for a while. Don't lose him though, I say, because your parents would really miss him.

In kids with AS/HFA, the editor is often asleep to begin with. Many times they end up in trouble, with their feet more in their mouths than out. What a relief, then, to have a place where they can be praised for not using their editor.

And so we move on to group storytelling and all its variations. By now, you will be over halfway through your classes and you will have a great rapport happening between your students. This is good, because verbal improvisation, while fun and rewarding, can also be scary and frustrating. Your kids will need to lean on each other. During the teaching of these exercises, you will be less of a goofy playmate and more of a teacher and director. You are moving toward a time when these students will be able to handle a small play. In order for that to be a success, you need to start preparing them for the rigors of that now.

The first thing to do when introducing the concept of group story is to have the group try to tell one. Sit in a circle and say,

"Tell me a story." It will be either long or short, but trust me, it will be lousy. And the kids will know it, too.

Explain to the group that a good story needs focus. Ask the group to name a famous person, a place and an object. Take the first three. Let's say it's Sponge Bob Squarepants™, Cincinnati, and a cheese grater.

Start the group by saying:

THIS IS THE STORY ABOUT SPONGE BOB
SQUARE PANTS, CINCINNATI, AND A CHEESE
GRATER.

This is the story you will get.

Once upon a time there was a guy named Sponge Bob and he lived in Cincinnati. And he had a cheese grater. The End.

Then, ask your students if they thought that was a good story. They won't. Explain to them that a good story has to have some surprise and suspense. If they put all that information in there right away, what else will they have to say? Tell them that this time, each person only gets to say one sentence at a time as they go around the circle. They can't introduce one of the three key components of the story until they have gone around the circle once. After that, they have to wrap up the story in two more turns.

Yes, you're right. This is tough. Don't beat this exercise into the ground. Intersperse some fun, movement exercises in between a few tries to keep things loose and fun. But don't lower your standards for a good story. Raise the bar and keep it there. Plan on spending a few sessions working on getting them to reach it.

Here is an example of how your first fledgling stories may sound:

You: THIS IS THE STORY OF PIKACHU, ENGLAND, AND A HAMMER.

Student A: Once upon a time, there was a hammer.

You: Try not to start off with one of your key elements.

Student A: Okay. I went away from home once.

Student B: and I decided that I would build a house.

You: Good. You added something to the story that makes it easy for someone else to incorporate a key element.

Student C: But I didn't have any tools. So I couldn't build a house, so I just laid down on the ground and

You: One sentence only.

Student C: But I didn't have any tools.

Student D: I don't know.

You: Okay. If you wanted to build a house and didn't have any tools, what could you do?

Student D: I don't know.

You: Could you ask someone for tools?

Student D: I guess so.

You: So say that.

Student D: I asked someone for tools.

Student E: But they couldn't help.

Student F: So I died.

You: Okay, if you die, that would be the end of the story. Try something else.

Student F: So I didn't DIE!

Student A: I found a mouse.

Student B: And his name was Pikachu.

Student C: And he said he knew where were some tools.

Student D: I don't know.

You: Well, what tool could he find?

Student A: A HAMMER!

You: Let him come up with it.

Student D: A hammer.

You: So say that.

Student D: So he gave me a hammer.

Student E: And then we built the house.

Student F: And we lived in the house and battled Charmander.
The End

You: Not bad you guys, but that was kind of an abrupt ending and you forgot about England. But we're getting there. Let's do it again with different things.

As I said, this is a tough exercise. But they will get it, and when they do, they'll have a wonderful sense of accomplishment.

Variations:

Students form small groups of 4 or 5. They stand in line and face the audience. You crouch in front of them. The group or the audience provides three key components: person, place and object. The story begins with the student you point to first. This student continues telling the story until you point to someone else. Once the finger is moved from a student, they must immediately stop speaking, even if they are in the middle of a sentence. Even if they are in the middle of a word. The next student pointed to must continue the story exactly where the last student left off, without missing a beat. Tell your students they must focus on "the fickle finger of fate" if they wish to tell a cohesive and convincing story. It is very entertaining to watch students finish each other's syllables and sentences, picking up a silly character voice from the person speaking before them. Make sure you hold them to the rules of the simple group story.

Mirror Story

Students form pairs. One at a time, each pair tells a story to the audience, using the mirror technique. The pair stands in front of the audience, facing each other. Student "A" is the leader, student "B" is the mirror. "A" will tell the story with words and gestures, while "B" mirrors and follows as closely as possible. Always begin the story with "ONCE UPON A TIME." It is also best for the pair to tell a very well-known story. Have the students review the rules for the regular mirror exercise. Remind the leader to go slow and make their body movements and inflections very big. "B"s should try to speak and move at the same time with no audible lags. Be prepared for lots of giggles at first, but eventually get them to really focus.

As pairs get better at this, you can call out "SWITCH" and have "B"s take over the lead in mid-story. You may want to challenge advanced actors by having pairs make up their own stories, or eliminating the role of a leading story teller.

Some final tips about storytelling. The kids know a good story when they hear one, but they may not know why it's good. It is important to choose components that are as dissimilar as possible. Queen Elizabeth in Buckingham Palace with a crown isn't nearly as interesting as if the Queen showed up in a bowling alley with a Christmas tree ornament. Tell your students to give themselves a challenge.

The real key to telling a group story is for students to listen carefully to the story unfolding without planning too far ahead in their minds. If Emmie is listening to Dana tell a story about ballet slippers and decides when she gets control of the story, there will be an elephant in a tutu, when the fickle finger of fate chooses her, that is all she'll be able to think to say. While she was daydreaming about her contribution, the story went off in a completely different direction. Then, Emmie has two choices, either force her idea into the plot or freeze and say nothing. Neither makes for a good story.

Creating a Character

Every exercise is a means of being able to create a character. This one, however, is straight and to the point.

Have your students get in groups of six. One of the students will be the performer. The other five will give him characteristics, like the good fairies did in *Sleeping Beauty*.

1. a walk

2. a gesture

3. a laugh

4. a voice

5. a sentence that starts with "I want"

Each person gives the performer their gift, having the performer practice until they are perfect. It is a good idea to make the performer one of your student aides the first time through. The performer then displays their character for the class.

Variations:

After the performer shows their character, each member of the team must perform it as well. Keep this a secret, and spring it on them. Hee, hee, hee.

Status

Status refers to one's standing on the social hierarchy. To use broad examples, the dominant male lion is the highest status animal in his pride. Cinderella has the lowest status in her household. Identifying a character's status, whether it be in a two minute skit or a two hour play, adds realism and entertainment value to an actor's performance. Entire books are written on how to portray and shift status during a scene. For our purposes, however, it is best to keep it simple.

Body Movements and Positions of High Status Characters

- Erect torso

- Exposed neck and chest

- Wide stance

- Relaxed, open body

- Leaning in and over

- Direct focus

- No wiggling, tapping

- Steady eye position (either eye contact or looking away)

Vocal Characteristics and Speech Patterns of High Status Characters

- Loud

- Clear

Steady sound (if the character says "um" or "er," the noise is drawn out until the next word. HS characters like to take up the space around them, even with sound).

- No stuttering

- Crisp diction

- Free, relaxed tone of voice

- Confident

- Proud

High Status characters never look truly worried. Concerned for others, perhaps, but not for themselves. They never question whether people like them or want to listen to them. They expect other people to do the things they tell them to. They believe themselves to be superior. They can vary from benevolent monarch to screaming tyrant. Do not assume the biggest or most powerful person in the room is the HS character. The screaming baby or a whining invalid can command a room. The lowliest beggar can conduct himself with as much High Status as the Queen of England.

Body Movements and Positions of Low Status Characters

- Concave torso

- Protected head and neck

- Twisted or crumpled body

- Weight off balance

- Body takes up as little space as possible

- Wiggling, tapping, general jumpiness

- Indirect eye contact, glancing around, constant breaking of eye contact

Vocal Characteristics and Speech Patterns of Low Status Characters

- Soft

- Weak

- Mumbling

- Apologetic

- Nervous

- Unfinished thoughts or sentences

- Short "uhs" and "ers"

- Stuttering

Low status characters try to take up as little space as possible. From the above description, you may assume that all low status characters are basket cases. Many are, but not all. Imagine not only the frightened employee caught photocopying his fanny by the president of the company, but also the smooth butler who facilitates his employer's every move without even being noticed in the room.

These attributes are all described in the extreme. Real people are usually much more subtle about displaying their status. Working with status can make people feel uncomfortable, especially if they are asked to portray a status that is foreign to them. My students frequently get off track by telling me about things that happened to them at school, because behaving as a low status character reminds them of their daily lives. Sadly, many children with Asperger's Syndrome have a lot of experience with feeling low status in social settings. I encourage these types of discussions, and often let a kid play out a scenario that mirrors a situation that he has experienced. First, we do it with the kid as low status.

Two kids on the play ground approach our student.

Our student looks nervous.

Two kids- Hey retard, why don't you go sit with the other retards in the retard trailer?

Our student hangs his head, mumbles or says nothing.

Two kids- Oh, I guess you're too RETARDED! laugh, walk away.

Our student sits and looks sad.

I know what you are thinking. Yes, "retard" is an ugly word, but it's one our kids hear said by bullies. When a kid is brave enough to volunteer his personal life as a situation to be discussed in acting class, the least I can do is let them make the scene as real as possible.

Okay, I say, excellent portrayal of low status. And that's what happened? Boy, that must have felt pretty lousy. Let's do that again, but this time, I want you to respond to them in some high status way. Even when you see them coming, don't curl up. Instead, open up and have that strong torso thing going on. Sometimes that's enough to make jerks like that take off, but even if it isn't, you are starting from a strong place.

Ordinarily, when a student is given an opportunity to confront his social attackers in a safe setting, he indulges his fantasy of being nasty or even violent to them. Be ready for this, and remind your student that although it may be tempting to shout and bully their tormentors, that never really works out in the end. Tell your student that adopting a high status body and voice may not make the kids stop completely and it may not make teasing feel okay completely, but it will take the edge off and end the situation more quickly.

Two kids approach our student.

Our student turns and makes direct eye contact with them.

Two kids wander off.

or

Two kids approach our student.

Our student purposely stays involved in what he is doing.

Two kids- Hey retard. Why don't you go sit with the other retards in the retard trailer?

Our student picks up his things and calmly walks away, never looking at the two kids.

Our student looks at me and says, "Hey, I thought I should always look at people when they talk to me." I say, "Kid, some people don't deserve your eye contact. They just aren't worth it."

or

Two kids approach our student.

Our student makes steady pleasant eye contact.

Two kids- Hey retard …

Our student- using clear, confident body language-
Leave me alone. I'm busy.

 If the situation is too upsetting for the kid to actually perform in, but he still wants to work through it, have actors perform the scene while the student directs.

 Again, high status body language and tone of voice won't fix everything, but it does help.

 To teach status, go back to the description of how to make a peanut butter and jelly sandwich. Have each student give brief instructions on how to make a PB&J, as either a high status or low status character. Have the class guess what each student performs and identify the specifics of each performance.

 Have students give same instructions, but shift to the opposite status somewhere during their speech. Tell the class to notice how much more interesting it is to watch someone change their status than just stay the same. This is another one of those sneaky acting secrets. Audiences like to see character progression in an actor's performance.

Variations:

Have students pair up. Give each pair a card that has two characters on it as well as the status of each one. The pair will devise some brief kind of situation and dialogue that shows the status of each character. Remind the students that even though they are working on status in this exercise, they must remember to incorporate their character's goals into the scene, as they did during their gibberish scenes.

Once each pair has performed, tell the class to keep their characters, but swap their status. Each pair will perform again, altering their small scene to incorporate the new status of each character. Here is an example:

A customer-High Status

A waiter-Low Status

The customer shows his high status while pointing out that the waiter has forgotten to arrange the customer's food in neat sections on the plate. The waiter humbly apologizes, then accidentally spills the plate of food in the customer's lap. The waiter grovels for forgiveness.

This same group will then swap their status this way.

A customer-Low Status

A waiter-High Status

The waiter walks up to the customer, asking for payment of the customer's bill. The customer realizes that he has left his cash at home. He tries to use his credit card, but it is declined. The waiter makes him wash dishes to pay for his bill.

Although both scenarios have the potential to be funny, you will notice that the kids will laugh more at the second one, especially if the customer played very high status in the first scene. This, tell your fledgling actors or actlings, as I like to call them, is because people enjoy seeing high status people laid low and low status people catch a break. There is nothing funny about seeing a small baby fall into a fountain at the park, but it is definitely funny to see a beautiful supermodel fall in that same fountain. It's even funnier to see her fall if she just yelled at her assistant and made him cry.

Here are some good pairs of characters to use for status exercises:

Teacher- HS

Student-LS

Teacher collecting homework, student hasn't done it.

Teacher-LS

Student-HS

Student asks a simple question the teacher doesn't know the answer to.

Doctor-HS

Nurse-LS

Doctor performing a difficult operation, nurse helping him.

Doctor-LS

Nurse-HS

Nurse catches doctor starting to perform the wrong operation on a patient. "Doctor Twimbly, you're trying to give Mr. Smith a hysterectomy!"

Famous Actress-HS

Dresser-LS

Actress needs the dresser to prepare her for the Academy Awards.

Famous Actress-LS

Dresser-HS

Actress has terrible body odor. Dresser is disgusted.

In a standard acting class, the teacher should push the students to come up with their own dialogue, allowing them to become frustrated and then push through their frustration to find creativity. With our kids, the actual portrayal of these characters is challenging enough, so if you see a group stall, don't hesitate to ask leading questions, give them ideas, and even script for them.

Commedia dell'Arte

There is a natural progression from discussing comedic status exercises to discussing Commedia dell'Arte. Commedia is an ancient form of comedic improvisation that originated in Italy as clowning and street theater. Its broad style and stock characters have influenced everything from the comedies of Shakespeare and Molière to early American vaudeville and modern day sitcoms. If you have an advanced acting class, you may want to read up on commedia and work on some small scenes. An excellent book filled with small scenarios is *Lazzi, The Comic Routines of the Commedia dell'Arte*, by Mel Gordon. The majority of commedia work is done through improvisation, meaning that the actors have a general guideline, but no set script. They know their characters and the plot line, their goals for each small scene, but they have to come up with dialogue and action themselves. True improv has this occur live, right in front of an audience, as in the show *Whose Line Is It Anyway?* with Drew Carey. In acting class, you hand the actors their characters, their plot line for a scene, and give them five-ten minutes to come up with something. Then, the class watches each scene and gives suggestions on how to improve the work. You may not be able to do this with every group of kids. It requires a lot of focus, creativity and confidence. I have included this information plus character descriptions and an original scenario in case you happen upon a motivated group. It is a lot of fun. It is rewarding to get a laugh from someone when you say a funny line. It is twice as rewarding if you came up with that line yourself.

Each Commedia has archetypical characters and situations that are immediately recognizable to the typical audience. Most of us recognize "the young lovers," the "evil miser," the "wise and crafty servant" and the "vain dignitary". The performance of these characters relies heavily on exaggerated body language, tone of voice and objectives. Our kids get a good skill workout not just by performing these characters, but identifying them as well. Recognizing and using nonverbal cues is a core challenge to students with AS\HFA. Working with the exaggerated tone of voice, body language and facial expression cues in Commedia is an excellent way for students to gain competence in this area. Here are some of the most popular characters:

Pantalone- Old man. Cheap and greedy miser. Foolish and often duped by those he employs.

Harlequino- A servant. Acrobatic and agile, but not very bright. Mischievous.

Doctore- Old man. Pompous and often boring to others. Pretends to know more than he does. Greedy.

Columbina- Intelligent, pretty, charming servant. A master schemer.

Fichetto- Clumsy, inept servant.

Celia- A young, beautiful girl, a lover. Perhaps a bit bubble headed.

Oratio- A young, beautiful boy, a lover. Perhaps a bit bubble headed.

The Captain- A vain, boastful soldier who is usually revealed to be a coward.

Ruffianna- A gossipy old woman.

Have the class work on the characterization of a character together. It doesn't matter the age or sex of the student, each one of them has to find a way to perform this character. Start with walking around the room, finding how the character walks. Remind them of the exercise where they had to be led by a certain body part. A lover might be led by his chest or heart, while a glutton might be led by his stomach or his nose. Explore how these characters might speak. Get the kids to think of modern day TV or movie characters that fit the description of the Commedia characters and have the students listen and mimic them for character development. Talk about what goals this Commedia character might have and how the character would go about achieving those goals. Come up with the top three tactics that this character would employ to get what he\she wants. Perhaps a sweet pretty girl would first flirt, then pout and cry, then throw a temper tantrum. A clear example for people my age is Scarlet O'Hara from *Gone With the Wind,* but don't expect the kids to know who she is. This is when your student aides prove invaluable. They know all the most modern references and can help you to sound less dated.

Once everyone in class has mastered every character in body, voice and mind, throw two separate characters into a simple scene with the same objective.

- Both characters want the only cupcake.

- Both characters want to be loved by the audience.

- Both characters want to sit in the only chair.

- Both characters want the other one to sing a song.

Make sure that your students stay true to their characters so that we can almost anticipate what they will do next.

If your class likes Commedia and you want to stretch them a bit, try this extended scenario. As you can see, it is as detailed as any script, and would be suitable for a class only after they had completed one full ten week session of acting class, and perhaps a small scripted play.

The Elixer of Life

Scene 1

Pantalone realizes that he will someday die. He panics at the thought of having to leave his money to someone else. He decides to seek the Elixer of Life and remain immortal.

Scene2

Pantalone calls for Doctore and Fichetta. He argues with them over their price. Pantalone's niece Celia and the servant Columbina pass through. Doctore names Celia's hand in marriage as his fee for the Elixer of life. Pantalone agrees. Doctore orders Fichetta to create a beautiful wedding dress for his future bride. Fichetta agrees. Alone, Fichetta panics and tells the audience that she has no idea how to make clothing.

Scene3

Celia meets with Oratio. They declare their undying love for one another. They swear that they will marry, but they must find a patron who will help them elope.

Scene 4

Harlequino and Columbina discuss the mutual benefits they will receive if their masters marry. They decide to help.

Scene 5

Doctore tells Fichetta and audience that there is no Elixer of Life. He plans to string Pantalone with bogus treatments for years to come. He will tell Pantalone that in order for the Elixer to work, Pantalone must be "prepared," and that this will need to be paid for. Harlequino and Columbina overhear his plot.

Scene 6

Both servants contemplate telling Pantalone right away, but decide that it will be more fun to watch and see what happens.

Scene 7

Doctore and Finchetta perform silly and outrageous acts on Pantalone, "preparing him" for the elixer.

Scene 8

Split scene. In two separate areas of the stage, both lovers are made aware of their impending doom. The lovers alternately berate and then plead with their servants for help.

Scene 9

Celia goes to beg Pantalone to reconsider, making Columbina do all the real groveling so Celia's dress doesn't get dirty. Fichetta secretly tries to get Celia's measurements.

Scene 10

Oratio enters. Challenges Pantalone to a duel. Pantalone accepts, reminding the audience that he is in no danger because he possesses the Elixer of Life.

Scene 11

Doctore has heard of the duel. He tries to convince Pantalone to sign money over to him now. Tells Fichetta that the dress must be done by tonight. Fichetta assures him this is no problem, then agonizes over her plight with the audience.

Scene 12

Harlequino and Columbina decide that things have gone too far. They must save the day with a brilliant plan.

Scene 13

Fichetta gets volunteers from the audience to help her with the wedding dress. Audience members are asked to model different parts of the outfit.

Scene 14

Pantalone is gleeful over the fact that he will live forever. A knock is heard on the door and two cloaked figures (disguised Harlequino and Columbina) enter. They are specialists sent from Doctore, they say. They examine Pantalone in absurd and silly ways. As long as he never kills a member of his (Pantalone's) own family, they say, a teardrop of pure joy will cause him, Pantalone, to live forever. Pantalone rejoices but then panics because he doesn't know any happy people. The specialists say they know of a young couple that needs someone to house their elopement. If the girl is married here, she will shed tears of pure joy and Pantalone can have as many tears as he likes. Maybe even sell them. Pantalone agrees. He wants it done tonight, before the duel.

Scene 15

Harlequino is off to search for a priest on short notice. He can't find one, and he bemoans his fate to the audience. Doctore overhears him and decides to make a little extra money by pretending to be a priest. He approaches Harlequino, who hires him immediately.

Scene 16

Doctore clumsily marries the two concealed lovers. Celia and Oratio leave. Columbina yells at Harlequino for not filling the vial and sends him off at once before Pantalone comes.

Scene 17

Pantalone comes to get his medicine. Columbina stalls. Harlequino arrives with a large bottle of suspect looking liquid. Pantalone takes a large sip and says he's feeling better already.

Scene 18

Oratio returns for the duel. Things begin to look bad for Oratio because Pantalone cheats. Harlequino and Columbina protest, revealing the secret marriage and reminding Pantalone that Oratio is now a family member (albeit through marriage). If Pantalone kills him, the Elixer of Life will no longer work. Doctore starts to protest, but Columbina threatens to reveal his plot to steal money from Pantalone and his bogus impersonation of a priest. Doctore promises to keep quiet.

Oratio and Pantalone embrace. Oratio invites Pantalone to live at his palace rent free. All rejoice and exit except Doctore, who remains, fuming.

Fichetta triumphantly bursts on the scene with the completed wedding dress. Doctore hollers and chases her out of the theater.

The End

There is one final exercise that doesn't quite fit in any category, and yet it is the one I do during almost every class and rehearsal.

One to Twenty

Students form a circle. They take baby steps in until they are as close to each other as possible without damaging the circle. Make sure they are nice and snug. Students close their eyes. The group then counts to twenty in random order. No patterns may be established. Any overlaps sets the group back to the beginning.

Don't expect your group to get past five for quite awhile. Tell them they must keep their eyes closed and they must try to sense the energy of the group. This is a great exercise if you need to refocus the class or calm them down. Don't wimp out and let them go to just ten. The day they reach twenty is a great day for the group. Watering the exercise down only robs them of that experience.

This exercise may be particularly difficult for those students who have trouble with light touch. Balance the importance of close proximity with your students' tolerance level.

These exercises, with the exception of the Commedia exercises, will take you through 10 hours of acting classes. Probably more. It is important for the students to master one before you go on to the next. Each exercise is a step up and gives the students tools to succeed at the next. Schedule around six exercises per class period. Have the class break around 35 minutes into the period to take a five minute snack break. Pick up where you left off. It is a good idea to start each class with the same simple exercises to focus and orient your students. Good ones to use are Mirror exercises and ones that ask the class to move as a group. You can even have a small structured chat session before each class. This is a nice way to check out your students' moods and assess who might need a bit extra attention that day.

Your final class will be a run through of all the exercises while parents and friends either watch, or more preferably, participate. The performance part can be emphasized by having students introduce each exercise and teach it to the audience. You might want to have students explain the purpose of the exercise, or tricks to make it easier. Feel free to allow your students to read off cards, but encourage them to "wing it" if they feel brave.

Acting Terminology

Here is a list of acting terminology. I always teach my students a few terms every class. Some are serious, some not so. The kids really enjoy having secret actor-type vocabulary to use during class. And, if you go on to do a play with your students, you will find that their new knowledge comes in handy when you direct them.

These are in no particular order. Introduce them in your class when the time presents itself.

Cue

The line or action before your line or action. It signals you to get ready and act.

Beat

A moment of time on stage. You may be asked "Wait a few beats before you exit."

Bit

A small piece of comedic action.

Take it from the top

To begin the play or scene from the beginning.

Tech rehearsal

A dull but necessary rehearsal when the technical cues are rehearsed. Notoriously boring for actors. I tell my students that sitting through a tech rehearsal initiates them into the secret world of actors.

Green Room

A place where the actors hang out. Legend says that it is called a Green Room, regardless of color, because that is where actors are paid.

Upstage

This does not refer to direction of movement, but to the act of moving in a direction away from the audience while onstage. This causes the actor in the scene with you to have to turn away from the audience in order to play the scene. This takes away the focus from the other actor. It is considered a nasty thing to "upstage" another actor unless you have been directed to do so.

Actors may retaliate by putting worms in your costume
or locking you in your dressing room. It is referred to as
"upstage" because many stages are raked or slightly
lifted in the back.

Focus

This refers to the mental energy of an actor. To focus on
something is to give it all your mental energy. It also
refers to who the audience is looking at during a
performance. If Billy is giving a speech, he should have
focus from the audience. If John is onstage with Billy,
and John starts to wiggle or make faces, he is stealing
focus from Billy, and disrupting the scene. Not good.

Pick up the pace

Speed up the movement and lines in a scene or exercise.

Mark

To mark something is to go through the motions but with
less than performance energy.

Cheat out

Positioning the body and face toward the audience, even
if the scene is taking place directly across from the actor.

Notes

Notes are suggestions given by the director to the cast after a rehearsal or performance. In the interest of time, most notes are critical rather than complimentary. Directors frequently say, "If I told you all the good things you did, we'd never go home."

Take the note

To listen to constructive criticism and implement it without argument.

Stage manager

The person who runs everything, has every answer, can solve every situation from repairing a broken set piece to finding the director's lucky coffee cup. An actor's best friend.

On book

Using a script during rehearsal.

Off book

Lines memorized. Usually, a stage manager will sit "on book" for actors the first few days that they are no longer using scripts.

Line

An actor says "line," when they can't remember what to say next.

Break a leg

The traditional way to say "good luck" to an actor.

I'll be in my trailer

Dramatic hysteria, usually from temperamental actors. Very silly.

Line reading

The director speaks the line exactly the way it needs to be spoken and the actor mimics her. Actors don't like this, but it is occasionally very useful.

Backstage

Behind the set.

In the wings

At the edge of onstage, but still backstage. Actors often watch from the wings when their favorite sections of the show are being performed. Sometimes, actors make faces at the performers on stage, but this could incur the wrath of the director. Or, worse yet, the stage manager.

Blocking

The physical action on stage.

Leading lady/man

Actors who play characters that usually have a large part in a show. Leading actors have a certain style and charisma that help them carry a show.

Character actor

An actor that frequently plays comedic or highly characterized roles. Many times a character actor will play a character of a different age. Character actors add spice and excitement to a show.

Cameo appearance

A small but important role in a show, usually with one appearance in the performance. These are often highly coveted for their low workload and high audience approval rating.

Scene stealing

When one character elicits a huge audience response during a scene. This can be good or bad, depending on how the scene is supposed to go. Sometimes, a small bit will get audience approval, so actors will make the bit longer and more elaborate for more audience approval. It is up to the director to decide when things have gone too far.

Show stopper

A section of a play that elicits so much audience approval that the performers must acknowledge the audience's approval before the show can go on.

The show must go on

An old saying in the theater that means, no matter what happens, keep going.

Bad dress rehearsal, good performance

It may sound like something said to make nervous directors feel better, but this is actually true. Perhaps this is because actors, after making mistakes during a dress rehearsal, gain some extra focus.

Five minutes

This is what the stage manager says to actors to let them know that it is five minutes to performance. The correct response to the stage manager is "thank you, five," which lets the stage manager know that you heard him and the correct time.

Holding the house

Delaying the performance a few minutes to allow late audience members to take their seats.

Call

The time an actor must arrive before the performance.

Run through

Performing the play from beginning to end.

Dress rehearsal

Running the play with costumes.

Full dress

Running the play with costumes, hair and makeup.

Final dress

Running the play as if there were an audience.

Double take

A bit when an actor sees something, turns away, realizes what he has seen and looks again. Classic comedy.

Running lines

Memorizing lines by speaking them without full performance energy while someone sits on book.

Line through

The cast sits and runs lines for the whole play as a means of rehearsal.

Now that you and your students have worked so hard together, you may want to continue working with them by rehearsing a play. Set aside another 10 week block of time. Your script should be short and sweet. The structure of your rehearsals should be 30 minutes working on the exercises from the last ten weeks and 30 minutes working on the play. I have included plays that would prove suitable for a class with many different skill levels. Do not announce the performance of your play until you are sure your students are ready to perform. Have strangers pop in from time to time to watch rehearsal in order to get your young cast used to such distractions. Pepper your cast with student aides, but give the big parts to your higher functioning Asperger's students.

Here is a great way to cast your play. Send each child home with a short nursery rhyme written on a 3x5 card. Tell them that they have until next class to memorize it, create a character for it and prepare it for performance. During that next class, watch each performance carefully. After each child performs, ask them to use a different characterization (cheerleader, sea slug, tiger) without any preparation on their part. Take note of who memorizes well, who thought up a great character and who did well when you asked them to improvise (directability). You might even want to huddle up with parents and find out how each kid handled their assignment. Cast your play accordingly. The higher the skill and comfort level of the AS\HFA student, the bigger their part.

Block or stage the play first. Unlike a regular play, do not expect your actors to come up with their own ideas for where they should move. They may come up with very creative stuff eventually, but your job is to get the whole play blocked and running as soon as possible. There will be time to tinker later. Keep your blocking simplistic and clear. Don't bother to teach stage right, stage left, etc. That's just frustrating. If you are having trouble communicating to a student, hop right up there and show him. Say his lines and do his blocking, with him right behind you mimicking everything you do.

Once the play is blocked, run it every class, at least once. Spend time running lines with students as well. Several students can run lines at once with the help of your aides. Teach the kids a simple trick when they forget their lines. Instead of saying "Sorry, I forgot my line. Oh, I'm such a ding-bat," tell them to simply say "Line," and the stage manager will read them the line. My cast really generalized this rule. Once, one of my young actors was trying to tell me what he had learned that day in science class. He said "I think it was...I can't remember the name... Line!"

Run, run, run that play. Run it until they can perform it in their sleep. The more confident they are, the more likely they will be able to deal with the unexpected during a performance. Vary the requirements of your run through, just to keep it interesting. Make one run through like a VCR fast forward, with everyone doing their lines as quickly as possible, another run through must be done with funny accents or sporadic monkey noises. Just keep running through the play.

A few weeks before the performance, start practicing how to be quiet back stage. This is where I begin to be a picky Director. I tell my students that I am not interested in a performance by a bunch of cute kids. I don't want the audience to smile and say, "Awww. Wasn't that cute?" I want them to be speechless at our talent and our professionalism. So no noise back stage. At all. Start with sticking them back stage and requiring them to be silent for two minutes. Progress to three, seven all the way up to 10 minutes. If they can do that, they can stay quiet during the play. Once you are up to four or five minutes, don't leave them back there alone. They'll get lonely and depressed. Go back there and make silly faces, fart noises and say outrageous things to get them to crack up. They love it when they learn to stonewall you.

There is an old saying in the theater. "Bad dress rehearsal, good performance."

Ah, yes. I remember repeating that to myself as I inhaled a pint of Ben and Jerry's while watching my class. It was our dress rehearsal. Had I <u>ever</u> rehearsed this play? Had anyone <u>ever</u> known their lines? What happened to all those funny little bits the kids had come up with? Gone, gone. As was my confidence. What had I done? I was setting these poor disabled waifs to fail. They would probably be scarred for life. We were doomed.

Twenty-four hours and two more pints of ice cream later, I watched my audience of happy parents and friends file in and take their seats. Fools! Leave before it is too late, I thought. Save yourselves while you still can.

The lights went down, the lights went up, and I proceeded to watch a play that I had only imagined in my dreams. Every character was portrayed to perfection. Not a line dropped. Heck, they even held the action for laughs. Everything I had begged, scolded, wheedled and hollered for them to do had been done, and in such an effortless manner that I hardly recognized them. What a group of pros!

Really, I should have known. Actors are actors, no matter what. Actors always save their best stuff for the only time that's important. When there's an audience. Everything else is just marking time.

After the performance, make them feel as glamorous as possible. Encourage audience members to ask for autographs, take many pictures, give many bouquets. And as your class is taking its bows and hearing its praises sung to the rafters by delighted friends and family, they, those timid students you once saw walk through the door, will turn to you and ask "So, what are we doing next?"

Which, of course, is entirely up to you!

Have Fun!

Part 3

The Plays

The following plays were written by John Stamm. An actor, director and acting teacher, John has been kind enough to lend his wacky sense of humor to our group. We, in The Renegade Acting Company, salute you!

I suggest that you use *The Rabbit's Bride* and *Jack and the Bean Stalk* for your beginners, *Cinderella, the Sequel* for your more advanced kids and *Hansel and Grethel* for your most advanced kids. You may want to consider double or triple casting the roles of Hansel and Grethel, and the Witch having each actor do only a few scenes. This may sound a bit strange, but it cuts down on line memorization and is really very funny. The key is to make bold costume choices that remain the same for each actor and have a few broad and recognizable characterizations such as a specific voice or funny walk that each actor adopts. You are not trying to convince the audience that these are the same actors, just the same characters. The pace of each play should be fast and furious. Take a look at some of the old Bugs Bunny/Daffy Duck cartoons and go for that kind of wacky style. The plays have minimal stage directions so that your cast can add funny bits as they come up in rehearsal. Enjoy.

Oh, yes. We hope that you will use these plays and that they will be wonderfully successful. However, if you choose to charge your audiences and you make over ten thousand dollars, send us a box of chocolate.

Cinderella: The Sequel

Characters

Anastasia

Drusilla

The Stepmother

The Messenger

Fairy Godmother

Messenger's Assistant

The Maid

Scene 1. The Sister's Home.

Anastasia:	I can't believe that Cinderella has gone to marry the prince and all because our feet were too big.
Drusilla:	And too stinky.
Anastasia:	Speak for yourself.
Drusilla:	O.K.
Anastasia:	What will we do now? Who's going to do all the work around here?
Drusilla:	Not me.
Anastasia:	Not me. Look! Mother has fainted. Wake her up!
Drusilla:	I don't know how. Cinderella always did that.
Anastasia:	Get some water!
Drusilla:	From where?

Anastasia: From the kitchen, stupid!

Drusilla: I don't know where the kitchen is. Cinderella did that stuff.

Anastasia: Well, shake her or something.

Drusilla: Where's her "or something?"

Anastasia: Do this! Mother! Wake up!

Drusilla: Yes, Mother! Wake up!

Mother: Ow!! Stop that!

Anastasia & Drusilla: Sorry, Mother.

Mother: Tell Cinderella to get me some water. Now!!

Drusilla: But I don't know the way to the palace.

Mother: What??

Anastasia: Cinderella has left to marry the Prince. Remember, Mother?

Mother: Oh, yes I remember now. Our family always had huge feet!

Drusilla: And stinky too!

Mother & Anastasia: Speak for yourself.

Drusilla: O.K.

Mother: I'm not feeling well. I'm going to lie down in my room. Bring me some tea.

(Mother exits)

Scene 2.

Anastasia: You heard her. Get the tea.

Drusilla: I don't know where the tea is or how to make it. I've never made anything.

Anastasia: Not that again!
What are we going to do?

Drusilla: About what?

Anastasia: About everything!!

Drusilla: I can't do everything.
                          I don't even know where everything is.

Anastasia: You don't know where anything is!

Drusilla: I don't?

Anastasia: No!

Drusilla: O.K.

Anastasia: You make me crazy!

Drusilla: Hey! I made something!

Anastasia: I know what we should do.
                          We should hire a maid.

Drusilla: A maid?

Anastasia: Yes. A maid.

(Maid enters)

Maid: Did somebody call for a maid?

Drusilla: Wow! That was quick!
Make me a sandwich, I'm hungry.

Anastasia: Yes, and I'd like some soup with a salad
and mother would like some tea.

Maid: Whoa! Hang on to your horses, girls.
We haven't discussed my duties or my
wages yet.

Drusilla: What's that?

Maid: What's that? Well, what am I going to
do around here and how much will I be
paid?

Anastasia: Oh, well, you'll do everything. Feed
the animals, clean the barn, clean the
house, make the meals, do the laundry,
wash the dishes, and make the beds.
You'll live in a little dinky room with
mice, you'll never get a day off, you
won't get any money, and we'll be
mean to you all the time.
When can you start?

Maid: You're crazy!

Drusilla: No, I'm Drusilla and she's Anastasia.

Maid: Nobody would take a job like that!

Drusilla: Cinderella did.

Anastasia: Well, actually we made her do
          everything.

Maid: You make me sick!

(Maid exits)

Drusilla: Hey! I made something else.
          Now I can make two things.

(Mother enters)

Mother: Where's my tea?

Drusilla: I don't have it.

Mother: Huh?

Anastasia: We're still looking for it mother.

Mother: Well, I want lunch now, too. You two are gonna have to do all the work that Cinderella did around here.

Anastasia: Why don't we hire a maid?

Mother: Because we have no money. I spent it all on clothes so you two could go to all those balls. What was I thinking?

Drusilla: I don't know.

Mother: Get to work!

(Mother exits)

Anastasia: We have no money! Now what will we do?

Drusilla: All these questions are making my head hurt.

Scene 3.

Anastasia: Look! Glass slippers! Cinderella must have left them behind by accident.

Drusilla: Wow!

Anastasia: We can sell them and with the money
                       we can hire a maid.

(Fairy Godmother enters)

Fairy Godmother: Oh no you don't! Those belong to me.

Anastasia: Who are you?

Fairy Godmother: I'm the Fairy Godmother.

Drusilla: No, really, who are you?

Fairy Godmother: Give me those shoes or I'll turn you
                       both into frogs!

Anastasia: Here!

Drusilla: If you're the Fairy Godmother why
don't   you give us glass slippers too?

Fairy Godmother: Because you're both too selfish and
                       mean. You don't deserve any gifts.

Anastasia: Isn't there anything we can do to make
                       up for it.

Fairy Godmother: Well, you could try to be like Cinderella was. You could perform an unselfish act.

Drusilla: A what?

Anastasia: She means to do something for someone else.

Drusilla: My head is hurting again.

Fairy Godmother: That's right girls. If you can find a way to do something nice for someone maybe something nice will happen for you. But don't do something just for the reward, cause that won't work.
Ta. Ta.

(Fairy Godmother exits)

Anastasia: So, all we have to do is something nice for someone. No problem.

Drusilla: Yeah. (Pause) What is something nice?

Anastasia: We can make mother her lunch.
That's nice.

Drusilla:	I'll do it! Then I'll get to marry a prince, too!
Anastasia:	No, I'll do it!
Drusilla:	No, I'll do it!
Anastasia:	You don't even know where the kitchen is!
Drusilla:	So?
Anastasia:	And you don't know how to make lunch!
Drusilla:	So?
Anastasia:	So, you're stupid!
Drusilla:	Am not!
Anastasia:	Am too!
Drusilla:	Am not!
Anastasia:	This will never work. The Fairy Godmother said not to expect a reward. How can you do something nice without expecting a reward?

Drusilla: I don't know.

I don't even know where the kitchen is.

Scene 4.

(Messenger and his assistant enter)

Messenger: Here ye! Here ye!

We have a message from the palace!

Assistant: Yeah!

We have a message from the palace!

Anastasia &   Wow!
Drusilla:

Messenger: We are here to escort someone to come and live at the palace.

Assistant: Yeah! We're the escorts!

Anastasia: Wow! And we haven't even done a good deed yet.

Drusilla: Yeah! That Fairy Godmother doesn't know what she's talking about.

Anastasia: Why do you need someone at the palace?

Messenger: The King needs a girl to serve cheese and crackers at the balls.

Assistant: Yeah! Cheese and crackers! I love them!

Anastasia & Drusilla: You mean work?

Messenger: Yes. You will be the Royal Cheese and Cracker Girl.

Assistant: Did I tell you that I love cheese and crackers?

Messenger: Why don't you wait with the horses?

Assistant: I'll go wait with the horses. Bye!

Messenger: As I was saying, you will live at the palace, wear fancy clothes and when you're not serving cheese and crackers you get to watch the royal television.

Anastasia:	Oh boy! We get to live at the palace and wear fancy clothes!
Drusilla:	Yeah, and watch the royal television! We'll take the job! When can we leave?
Messenger:	Wait a minute. I didn't say anything about both of you. We only have room for one Royal Cheese Girl.
Anastasia & Drusilla:	Just one?
Messenger:	That's right.
Anastasia & Drusilla:	Oh.
Messenger:	I'm going to wait outside. Let me know what you decide to do.

(Messenger exits)

Anastasia:	That means that only one of us can live at the palace and one of us will have to stay here and wait on mother.

Drusilla:	Yeah. (Pause)
	I think you should go Anastasia. I'll stay here and wait on mother. I'm sure I'll find the kitchen eventually.
Anastasia:	No, I think you should take the job. I'm sorry I called you stupid.
Drusilla:	No, I'm sorry.
Anastasia:	No, I'm sorry.

(Enter Fairy Godmother)

Fairy Godmother:	Well, you did it!
Anastasia:	We did?
Drusilla:	What did we do?
Fairy Godmother:	An unselfish act.
Drusilla & **Anastasia:**	We did?
Fairy Godmother:	Yes, you did. And now I will reward you.

Drusilla: What do we get? Extra large glass slippers with Odor Eaters™?

Fairy Godmother: No.

Anastasia: Well, what?

Fairy Godmother: You'll see.

(Enter Messenger and Assistant)

Messenger: Hold everything! We just got a message! The king has decided to build a bigger ballroom. So now he needs two Royal Cheese Girls.

Assistant: Yeah! More cheese and crackers! Did I tell you …

Messenger, Fairy Godmother, Anastasia and Drusilla:
Yes! We know!
You love cheese and crackers!!

Assistant: I think I'll go wait with the horses.

(Assistant exits)

Messenger: Well, do you want the jobs?

Anastasia & Drusilla:	Yes! Oh thank you Fairy Godmother!!
Fairy Godmother:	Goodbye girls. Don't forget what you've learned here.
Drusilla:	We will. I mean, we won't. I think.
Anastasia:	Come on Drusilla. Don't you think those messenger boys are cute?
Drusilla:	Yeah! Especially the little one.

(Sisters exit)

(Enter Mother. Sees Fairy godmother)

Mother:	Who are you?
Fairy Godmother:	I'm the Fairy Godmother.
Mother:	Good for you. Well, don't just stand there. Get me my lunch. And when you're finished, clean the bathroom and then …
Fairy Godmother:	Lunch, huh? I hope you like flies.

(Turns Mother into frog)

Mother: Rivet, Rivet!!

Fairy Godmother: And they all lived happily ever after.

The End!

Hansel and Grethel

Characters

Hansel

Grethel

The Bird

Rapunzel

The Rabbit's Bride

Little Red Riding Hood and the Wolf

The Witch

Scene 1. The Scary woods.

(Hansel and Grethel enter)

Hansel:	Hey!
Grethel:	(Looking around) What? You found something to eat?
Hansel:	Hey!!!
Grethel:	We can't eat hay!
Hansel:	No! Look! (Points off.)
Grethel:	Wow! What a big bird!
Hansel:	Yeah and he ate the trail of crumbs I left behind us so that we could find our way out of this forest!!
Grethel:	So much for that idea. You might as well save the rest of the crumbs for us.
Bird:	Cheap!
Hansel:	What did he say?

Grethel: He cheeped. How cute.

Bird: Cheap! Cheap!

Grethel: Awww, he must think I'm his mother.

Bird: No, I think you're cheap!

Hansel & Grethel: Huh? Whaaaa!

Bird: It's bad enough that you toss down these diet cracker crumbs. So now you're just gonna stop?

Grethel: Wow!! A talking bird!

Hansel: Maybe we shouldn't have eaten those berries.

Grethel: Yeah.

Bird: Looks like you two could live a month off all that Swiss cheese you must have eaten.

Hansel: We're not Swiss, we're German!

Grethel: O.K. Let's not bring our heritage into this.

Hansel: Look, Bird dude, could you help us find our way out of this forest?

Grethel: Yeah, we're kind of lost.

Bird: Kind of?

Grethel: O.K. Mister Exactomundo, we're completely lost.

Hansel: Yeah, our folks took us out here and left us with just a few cracker crumbs. And now we can't find our way back home.

Bird: Why did they do that?

Grethel: They said there wasn't enough food for all of us and that we'd have to fend for ourselves. Nice parents, huh?

Bird: Looks like you two were eating them out of house and home.

Hansel: We don't eat that much, although you sure would look good with some mashed potatoes and stuffing.

Bird: Back off tubbo. This beak's not just for talking.

Grethel: I blame the fast food companies. They just make those quarter pounders taste too good.

Hansel: My downfall was the curly fries.

Grethel: And those milkshakes, and the tacos that they sell two for a buck, and the little chicken pieces with the dipping sauce, and those messy burgers that drip everywhere, and that really cold ice cream that the astronauts eat and...Hey! where did the bird go?

Hansel: He either got hungry or bored, cause he left.

Scene 2.
Still in the forest. It's still scary.

Hansel: Man, this forest is scary.

Grethel: Ya, think?

Hansel: Hey!

Grethel: Not that again. I told you we're not
                     cows; we can't eat hay!

Hansel: No, look!

(They see Rapunzel, standing on a table.)

Grethel: Who are you?

Rapunzel: I'm Rapunzel.

Hansel: Are you the: "Rapunzel, Rapunzel, let
                     down your hair." Rapunzel?

Rapunzel: Yes, that's me.

Grethel: O.K. is that a literal thing or an idiom?
                     I mean when people tell you to let down

your hair, are they really just telling you to loosen up a bit and have some fun?

Hansel: Or, do they mean to actually let down your actual hair?

Rapunzel: Whoa! Where do you guys come from? Switzerland or something?

Hansel: Huh? What's that supposed to mean?

Rapunzel: You just look like you've eaten a lot of Swiss cheese.

Grethel: See. I told you we shouldn't eat so much cheese.

Hansel: Well, we eat good old German cheese. The best cheese there is and …

Grethel: (Interrupts)
You never told us why people ask you to let down your hair.

Rapunzel: Well unless you've been living in the Alps you'd know that an evil witch stuck me up in this tower and the only way anyone can get up to me is to climb up my hair. Sooooo … that's where the "Rapunzel, Rapunzel, let down your hair" came from.

Grethel: But I thought there was something about a handsome prince who was supposed to rescue you?

Rapunzel: Yeah, well, that was an accident. He came not so long after I first grew my hair out and I couldn't hear so well cause I just had too much hair. So when he said: "Let down your hair." I thought he said: "Throw down your chair." And I tossed down my chair and hit him in the head. He hasn't been back since, the wimp.

Grethel: Bummer.

Rapunzel: You got that right. And now I'm stuck up here in this tower and the only visitors I get are the nasty old witch and some mouthy talking bird.

Hansel: Hey! We met that bird! He's rude. But, hang on a minute! What do you mean you're stuck up in that tower? You're

just standing on a table. You could just
get down and leave.

Rapunzel: Wow, and all these years I thought I
was trapped up here. See ya, cheese
heads.

(Rapunzel exits)

Grethel: Hey! Wait a minute! How about
helping us get out of here!

Hansel: She's gone.

Grethel: You know people sure are rude in this
forest. Not scary just rude.

Hansel: I sure am hungry.

Scene 3.
The no longer so scary, but rude forest.

Grethel: Look, someone is coming. A woman.

Hansel: How come no one else seems to be lost
in this forest except us?

The Rabbit's Bride: Hello.

Grethel: Who are you?

The Rabbit's Bride: They call me the "Rabbit's Bride."

Hansel: Whoa!

Grethel: Huh? Come again?

The Rabbit's Bride: A rabbit would come into my mother's garden everyday and eat her cabbage. Mother told me to go and shoo the rabbit away. But every time I did he would say: "Sit on my tail and go with me to my rabbit hutch." After the third day of me shooing him and his asking me to go, I said to myself: "Why not? It's boring here." So I went.

Hansel: Whoa!

The Rabbit's Bride: Well, after I got there I find out he wants to get married and have me cook cabbage all the time and I said: "No way." and he says: "Way." And I couldn't get out of there because he had all his rabbit friends around so I made a figure of me out of straw, put it in front of the stove where I had been cooking cabbage and I hid. Then he comes into the kitchen and tells me it's time to get married and when the straw figure didn't answer he pushed it and it fell over and he yells: "Ahhhh! I've killed her." and he ran out of the house. So I'm on my way back home.

Grethel: That is one messed up story.

The Rabbit's Bride: It may be, but it's my story and it IS an actual Grimms' Fairy tale.

Grethel: Whatever!
It's still one messed up story!

Hansel: You said it, Grethel. Hey! All this talk about rabbit is making me hungry again. Is he nearby? I could go for a good rabbit stew.

The Rabbit's Bride: He's a six-foot tall rabbit. He'd knock you on your pudgy Swiss cheese fanny!

(The Rabbit's Bride exits)

Grethel: You know this is the weirdest forest I have ever been in.

Hansel: It's kind of like the Fairy Tale Twilight Zone.

(Enter Little Red Riding Hood.)

Red Riding Hood: Hello, could you tell me the way to Grandma's house?

Hansel & Grethel: No!!!

Red Riding Hood: Wow, how rude.

(Red Riding Hood exits)

(Enter Wolf)

Wolf: Hey, Waazzup! Did you see a little Red Riding Hood?

(Hansel points offstage. Wolf exits)

Grethel: Hansel, look! Is that a house?

Hansel: (Still staring after wolf) Huh?

Grethel:	Look it's a house! Made out of ginger bread! And the roof is made out of cakes and the windows are made out of transparent sugar!
Hansel:	Girl, you have finally lost your German marbles.
Grethel:	No! Look!

(Hansel looks towards the house and a "dum da da DUM!" is heard.)

Hansel:	Wow, it is a house! But what was that noise?
Grethel:	That was a "dum da da DUM!" It means something big just happened.
Hansel:	Oh.
Grethel:	Come on! Let's eat!

Scene 4.
Outside the House.

Hansel: Munch, munch, chew, chew.
Man, this wall is great!

Grethel: You should try some of this windowsill.
I think it's French pastry.

(They hear a voice from within.)

Voice: "Nibble, Nibble like a mouse,
Who is nibbling at my house?"

(Hansel and Grethel look at each other.)

Hansel: "Uh … Never mind.
It is the wind."

Grethel: (Gives Hansel a thumb's up and
whispers) Good one. Hee, hee.

Hansel: (Whispering) Pretty slick, huh?

Witch: (Entering) Wind huh? The only wind
around here is from you two farting
around!!

Hansel and Grethel: Ahhhh!!

Witch: Now, now, don't freak out on me. It's okay. Kids get hungry, they gotta eat. I just would like to avoid having a hole in my wall that's all.

Grethel: Um … excuse me. But, why did you make your house out of food? I mean, wouldn't the birds eat your roof and all?

Witch: Such a lovely child, such a precious child! Well dear, you see, it's because my whole life revolves around food and eating. My house is a celebration of food and food products. My name is Genny Kake and I run a diet food corporation.

Hansel: Awesome!

Witch: Yes, my chunky dear, it is awesome! I help people break those nasty eating habits that lead to things like pudginess and sloth-like behavior. I see that you two found me at just the right time.

Grethel: Oh, so you built your house out of ginger bread and candy and stuff to lure people here so you could help them lose weight.

Witch: Such a brilliant child! Go to the head of the class. Straight "A's" for you sweetie. You're the Magna Cum Laude of …

Grethel: O.K! We get the picture.

Hansel: Sorry about chowing on your house, Geenie.

Witch: It's Genny dear, and don't you two worry your plump little brains.
I'll baste you … I mean I'll bet you are still hungry right? How about we see what there is to eat inside?

(Witch exits)

Hansel: Awesome!
This forest isn't so bad after all!

(Hansel exits)

Bird:	(from off stage) Cheap!!
Grethel:	It's still darn rude, though!

(Grethel exits)

Scene 5. Inside the House.

Witch:	Now my dears, we must do something about your weight.
Hansel:	Yeah we know, we're a little overweight.
Grethel:	Yeah, everyone in this forest has been on our case about it. What's up with that, anyway? Is this some kind of weight watchers wooded whiner wasteland?
Hansel:	Nice alliteration Greth!
Grethel:	Thanks, Hans.
Hansel:	So what, do we have to eat a salad now?

Witch:	Oh no, dearies. You are mistaken. That's not the kind of diet program I run. Why do you think I'm called Genny Kake?
Grethel:	Cause that's your name?
Witch:	No, no, my dear. Here, maybe this will help. Our company motto is: Let them eat Cake! What do you think?
Grethel:	I don't get it.
Hansel:	Huh?
Witch:	Oh my precious, dears. You're not the sharpest knives in the drawer, are you? Well, let me explain. You see, our research experts discovered that the more sugary foods you eat the faster your metabolism moves and thus you will lose weight. So, on my diet we eat nothing but cakes, candies and pies.
Grethel:	That's like so unscientifically wrong.
Hansel:	Says the girl who flunked out of lab.

Grethel: Only because I wouldn't dissect the frog. He told me he was a prince. But I wouldn't kiss him and then Dorrie Evans dissected him and that was that.

Witch: Alright children, what shall it be? Tasteless salads, broccoli, and brussel sprouts or sweet, sugary cakes and candies!?

Hansel & Grethel: Cakes and candies, cakes and candies!!

Witch: What a surprise.

Scene 6.
Later. Still in the house.

Hansel: You know Grethel, I'm getting sick of all this junk food.

Grethel: Yeah, I never thought I'd say it but I'm starting to crave cauliflower. In fact I'm feeling like a crunchy cauliflower, cookie, crumble, cake!

Hansel: Okay, enough with the alliterations, already!

Grethel: Sorry. You know Hansel, something doesn't seem right about all this. We've been here three weeks now and I haven't lost any weight at all and neither have you. And Genny keeps coming in every day and feeling my arm and saying: "Um hum. Almost there." I mean, what's up with that?

Hansel: Yeah, the other day she said to me. "What do you think about Thyme and Rosemary?" And I said: "Are they that Norwegian Techno-pop band from Oslo?" And she just laughed. I mean it was spooky.

(The Witch enters)

Witch: Helloooo, my succulent dearies. Mind you, I've misplaced my contact lenses and I can't see very well so you might have to help me with a few things. Now, where is my juicy little Hansel? I need to check your plumpness … er …

I mean, check your weight. Hold out
your arm, there's a good boy.

Hansel:
(Whispers to Grethel)
Greth, check this out.

(Hansel holds out a wooden spoon handle for the witch to feel.)

Witch:
What's this? You've lost weight! Oh
no, that won't do! That won't do at all!
What have you been doing?
Exercising, or something like that?
Well? Speak, boy!

Hansel:
(Laughing to himself)
Whoa, chill Mrs. Kake. I think the
metabolism thing you were talking
about has kicked in. I must have eaten
enough sugar and now I'm losing
weight.

Witch:
What! Don't be an idiot! That doesn't
work ... uh ... I mean, that doesn't
work until the week we add the ice
cream. There now, my little buttercup,
you keep eating and let me check dear
young Grethel.

Grethel: (Laughing at what her brother did)
Haw, haw, haw!!

(The witch grabs Grethels' arm)

Grethel: Hey, Owww!

Witch: Perfect! You're ready now my dearie.
Hee, hee, hee!

Hansel and Grethel: Ready for what?

Witch: For dinner of course. I've been
fattening you up for a feast. My feast!
Hee, hee, hee!

Hansel & Grethel: Gross!

Witch: Yes, I know it's not very politically
correct, but I'm an old school witch
and, well, I can't help it. I just like
eating children. Sorry.

Hansel & Grethel: That's okay. Wait! I mean, gross!

Grethel: Hansel, run for it!

Hansel: I can't! My legs won't work!

Witch: Yes, Hansel dear, I put a spell on your legs so that you wouldn't be able to run away. Hee, hee. I should have done that to my first husband, the bum. Now Grethel, to the kitchen with you!

(Takes Grethel by the arm and leads her offstage.)

Grethel: Eeeeeek!!!

Hansel: (Tries to move)
You bogus witch! Grethel! Tell her you don't taste good! Tell her you taste like … like … like brussel sprouts! Gee, maybe she likes brussel sprouts. I know! Grethel tell her you taste like … like a mayonnaise, chocolate ice cream and dill pickle smoothie! Actually, I tried that once and it wasn't bad. Grethel, tell her you taste like, let's see, uh … oh this has to work! Grethel tell her you taste like worms and horseradish with peanut butter an inch thick on top!

(Grethel enters)

Grethel: Ooookay, you can stop now!
That was really disgusting!

Hansel: Grethel!!!!

Grethel: Yeah?

Hansel: You're not eaten!

Grethel: I know.

Hansel: What happened?
Where's Genny the Kake witch?

Grethel: She's toast!

Hansel: Oh, gross! Don't tell me you ate her?

Grethel: Oh, get real, Bozo. I'm no cake lady.

Hansel: Hey, my legs work again! The spell is
gone! What did you do to her?

Grethel: Well, we got in the kitchen and she
goes: "Well, missy you need to get into
that microwave oven." and I go: "Nah,
ahh!" And she goes: "Uh, huh! Cause
I'm going to microwave your sorry

self." And I go: "No way, cause I won't fit in there!" And she goes: "Oh yes you will!" And we both go: "Gross!!" Cause we heard what you said and you were grossing us out. And then I go: "How am I supposed to fit in there?" And she goes: "You little twit, even I could fit in there!" And I go: "Nah ahh!" And she goes: "Could too!" And I go: "Could not!" And she goes: "Could …"

Hansel: (Interrupting) Holy hopping hotdogs! Will you tell me what happened????

Grethel: Whoa, nice alliteration. Well, then I tell her to show me and so she crawls into the microwave oven and I gave her a push and she went in all the way so I shut the door on her and pushed the popcorn time button.

Hansel: Whoa. Then what happened?

Grethel: She popped.

Hansel: Wicked!

Scene 7.
The witch's house. Six months later.

Grethel:

(On the phone)
Hello, Genny Kake Earthy and Crunchy enterprises. No … I'm sorry we don't sell anything with refined sugar anymore. Just natural fructose and organic honey. Yes that was the policy of the previous management but we've since discovered that the cake diet does not work. We're now the company with your eating health in mind. So can I put you down for a case of Tofu Twinkies? Great and just cause you're such a good customer I'm gonna throw in some of that Low Sodium Pickle smoothie mix … Oh no, it's no problem … sure don't mention it. (Hansel enters) Well, I've almost gotten rid of all that stupid smoothie mix of yours. The next time you want to invent a product check with me first, O.K.?

Hansel:

Yeah, yeah.   Hey, the wolf says he wants some more of those grandma shaped bran muffins, and the rabbits down at the hutch need 4 cases of the carrot surprise. Gee Greth, you know, I feel so much better since we stopped eating all that junk food and went macrobiotic.

Grethel: Yeah, I feel better, too, and I have to admit I don't find you half as obnoxious anymore.

Hansel: Speaking of obnoxious.

(The bird enters)

Bird: Alright, the bears down at the river want more frozen bean sprout peanut butter worm pies.

Hansel: See! That one sells!

Bird: They also want them by tomorrow for some big bushy bear bash.

Hansel & Grethel: Nice alliteration!

Bird: (Rolls his eyes)
Please. Look if I have to deliver that today how about some overtime.

Grethel: Sorry bird.
You had overtime last week.

Bird: Cheap!

Grethel: Hey, did you just call me cheap!

Bird: No, I cheeped. I'm a bird.
It's what I do.

Hansel: Well get going and make that delivery.

Bird: CHEAP! CHEAP!

Hansel & Grethel: Hey!

The End!

Jack and the Beanstalk

Characters

The Mother

Jack

The Cow

The Salesperson

The Giant

The Harp

The Goose

Scene 1. Jack's House.

Mother: Jack!! You lazy bum!
Get out here this minute!

Jack: O.K. Mom!

Mother: We need money. I want you to go to
town and sell this cow.

Jack: O.K. Mom.

Mother: And make sure you stay away from
those crooked sales people!

Jack: O.K. Mom.

Mother: And don't get lost like last time! (Exits)

Jack: O.K. Mom. C'mon, ya dumb cow.

Cow: Moo!

Scene 2. On the Road.

Cow: Moo!

Salesperson:	Howdy there!
Jack:	Howdy!
Salesperson:	That's a mighty fine lookin' cow ya got there, son.
Cow:	Moo!
Salesperson:	Yes, indeedy! A mighty fine cow. Is she for sale?
Jack:	Yep. I'm on my way to town to sell her for a good price. My mom needs money.
Salesperson:	Well sonny, this is your lucky day! I'll buy that cow and I'll even make you a special deal!
Jack:	Really?
Salesperson:	Yep. I'll give you these magic beans for your cow.
Jack:	Beans?
Salesperson:	Magic beans!

Jack: I'm not allowed to have any magical
                      things.

Salesperson: Well, I call them magic beans but
                      actually they're radioactive.

Jack: Oh. Well that's O.K. then.
                      Here's your cow.

Salesperson: Thanks, sonny.

Cow: Moo!

Scene 3. Back at Jack's house.

Jack: Mom! I'm home!

Mother: Did you sell the cow?
                      Where's the money?

Jack: I didn't get money, I got beans!

Mother: Beans?

Jack: And not just any beans, I got
                      radioactive beans!

Mother: Radioactive beans?

Jack: Yeah, they'll grow … uh …
                     well, … they'll be … Gee! I don't
                     know what they'll do.

Mother: Oh boy, you are one dumb kid!
                     Gimmee those beans! (Throws beans.)
                     Now go clean the barn!

(Mother exits)

Jack: Sorry.

Scene 4. Jack's House. (The next day.)

Jack: (Sees beanstalk)
                     Wow! It goes right up into the clouds!
                     I wonder what's up there? Well, there's
                     only one way to find out!

(Climbs beanstalk. Looks around.)

                     Wow! I can see my house and the
                     whole farm from up here! Hey, there's
                     a castle over there. I think I'll see who
                     lives there.

Scene 5. The Castle.

Jack: Hello, is anyone home? Hello! Hello!

Harp: Quit your yelling!
Do you want to wake the Giant?

Jack: Who are you?

Harp: I'm a magic harp.

Jack: You mean radioactive don't you?

Harp: Huh?

Goose: Honk! Honk!

Harp: Oh no! Now you've got that dopey
goose honking. That'll wake the Giant
for sure!

Jack: Hey! Are those golden eggs?

Harp: Yep. That goose lays golden eggs.

Jack: Wow!

Goose: Honk! Honk!

Jack: Wow! With this goose my mom can sell the eggs, and with this talking harp we can sell tickets so people can talk to it. We'll never be poor again.

Goose: Honk!

Harp: Help! Help!

Giant: Fee Fie Fo Fum! I smell the blood of an Englishman!

Jack: What was that?

Harp: That's the Giant.

Giant: Who are you and what are you doing with my goose and harp?

Jack: I just wanted to borrow them for awhile. I didn't think you'd mind. Are you the Giant?

Giant: That's right!

Jack:	Well, you're not very big. You're just standing on that table.
Giant:	Oh yeah? They call me the Giant cause I have big feet.
Jack:	Wow, those are some big feet.
Giant:	Yeah and now you're gonna get it!
Jack:	Wait! Did you get the letter I sent you?
Giant:	Huh? No.
Jack:	Well, I must have forgot to stamp it. (Stamps on Giant's foot).
Giant:	Oww!!!!!
Jack:	C'mon Goose, c'mon Harp we're outta here!!

(Jack exits with Goose and Harp)

Giant:	I'll get you, and when I do I'm gonna stomp you into the ground!!

Scene 6. Jack's House.

Jack: I've got to chop this beanstalk down so the Giant can't follow me!! (chops down beanstalk).

Giant: Ahhhhhhhhhhh!!!!!! (Giant falls)

Jack and Harp: Wow!

Goose: Honk!

Mother: (Comes out of house) Jack! What's all that noise?

Jack: Nothing Mom. Just a giant falling.

Mother: What's all this?

Jack: Well, it's a long story Mom. This is a goose that lays golden eggs and this is a talking harp.

Harp: How ya doin'?

Goose: Honk!

Jack: We're gonna be rich!

Mother: Jack, you're not such a dummy after all.

Giant: (waking up)
Ohh. My head! What happened?

Jack: You fell from up there.
Sorry about that.

Giant: That's okay. I don't blame you.
I've been very grumpy lately.
That bump on the head has done me a world of good. Hey that's my goose and harp!

Jack: Yeah. Do you want them back?

Giant: No, you keep them. They were too noisy, especially the Harp. I'm gonna travel around for awhile. Maybe try out for a women's basketball team. I've got the feet for it. Well, bye.

(Giant exits)

Mother:	Well, that's enough sitting around Jack. Time to get back to work!
Jack:	O.K. Mom.
Mother:	I want you to get rid of that beanstalk lying there.
Jack:	O.K. Mom.
Mother:	And then clean the barn! C'mon Harp, c'mon Goose! Time for you two to get to work, too!
Jack and Harp:	O.K. Mom.
Goose:	Honk! Honk!

The End!

The Rabbit's Bride

Characters

The Mother

The Daughter

The Rabbit

The Rabbit's Friends

The Crow

Amelia Davies

Scene 1. The Cabbage Garden.

(Enter Mother)

Mother: Oh dear, oh dear!

(Enter Daughter)

Daughter: Oh Mother! What ever is wrong?
It distresses me so to see you so
unhappy.

Mother: It's that rascally rabbit! He's eating our
cabbages again! Oh dear!
Could you please go into the garden and
drive out the rabbit?

Daughter: Of course Mother! I will do anything
you ask. You are my mother after all. I
will shoo that pesky rabbit.

(Exits)

Mother: Such a sweet girl. But she's a bit too
agreeable. That may cause problems
for her someday. Sigh!

(Exits)

Scene 2. The Cabbage Garden.

(Enter Daughter. Looking down at the ground.)

Daughter: Now where is that rabbit? Shoo, shoo!
                       Don't eat up all our cabbages little
                       rabbit!

(Enter Rabbit)

Rabbit: How you doin'?

Daughter: (Looks up at rabbit.)
                       Oh my.   You're a very big rabbit.

Rabbit: Well, it's due to your excellent
                       cabbages. Say you're one very pretty
                       young lady.

Daughter: (Blushes) Tee hee! Nuh, uh!

Rabbit: I mean it. You are the prettiest maiden I
                       have ever seen in a cabbage patch.

Daughter: Tee, hee! Stop it! Really?

Rabbit: Really! You're even prettier than Farmer Bob's Scarecrow and that's saying something around here.

Daughter: Wow!

Rabbit: Would you like to go with me to my rabbit-hutch? My friends and I are having a party.

Daughter: Gee, I don't know.

Rabbit: C'mon. It'll be fun! And you can be the guest of honor!

Daughter: The guest of honor? Okay!

(Both Exit)

Scene 3. The Rabbit-Hutch.

(Enter Rabbit and Daughter)

Rabbit: Well, here we are.

Daughter: Wow, you have straw all over your floor.

Rabbit: Yes, the straw makes the floor softer to hop on. Say, my guests will be arriving soon. Could you do me a favor?

Daughter: Sure.

Rabbit: Could you cook some bran and cabbages in the kitchen. I'm going to bid the wedding …er …the party guests welcome when they arrive.

Daughter: Okay!

(Enter Rabbit friends)

Rabbit Friend 1: Hey! What's on the tube today?

Rabbit Friend 2: Let's watch the rabbit escape races again!

Rabbit Friend 3: Yeah! I just love watching the rabbit get away from those greyhounds!

Rabbit Friend 2: Yeah! The greyhounds never catch him.

Rabbit Friend 1: I always thought those racing rabbits were too stuck-up. I mean they never

interview after the races. What's up
with that?

Rabbit: And they're really stiff looking during
the race.   I bet they make more carrots
in one race than we do in a whole year.

Rabbit Friend 3: You got that right! (Grabs TV guide)
Let's see what's on. There's:
"Everybody Loves Rabbit."

All other Rabbits: Naw! It's a repeat.

Rabbit Friend 3: "Real Rabbit World."

All other rabbits: Naw!

Rabbit Friend 3: Hey, guess who's on "Late Night with
Peter Cottontail?"

All Rabbits: Who? Who?

Rabbit Friend 3: Our favorite comedian!!

Rabbit Friend 1: Who's that?

All other Rabbits: Carrot Top!! Who else?

Rabbit Friend 2:   What's your favorite color?

All Rabbits: Orange!

Rabbit Friend 3:   Hey, look what starts in an hour!

All other rabbits: What? What?

Rabbit Friend 3:   Watership Down!!

All other rabbits: No way! Oh, that's the best movie ever made! I love that movie! Yeah! Go Fiver!

(Daughter enters)

Daughter: What do you want me to do with the cabbages when they're done?

Rabbit: Just leave them on the stove for now and bring out the plates of carrot surprise.

Daughter: Alrighty! (exits)

Rabbit Friend 1:   Who was that?

Rabbit: That's my fiancé.

All Rabbit Friends: Say what? Huh? Whoa!

Rabbit: Yep. I decided that it was about time that I had someone around here to take care of things.

Rabbit Friend 3: Why don't you get a maid?

Rabbit: Too expensive.

Rabbit Friend 2: Did you get her a ring?

Rabbit: 8 karats.

All Rabbit Friends: Sweet! Whoa! Classy!

Rabbit: Thanks! Look the parson will be here soon. Why don't you guys watch TV in the jumping room and I'll call you when we're gonna start.

(Rabbit Friends exit. Enter Crow. The Parson.)

The Crow: CAW! CAW!

(Enter the Daughter)

Daughter: Oh my! What's that loud noise?

Crow: CAW! CAW! Sorry. I was helping myself to some snacks from your trays by the front door and I got some nuts stuck in my throat. CAW! CAW! Well, where are the wedding guests? When do we start?

Rabbit: They're in the jumping room. Why don't you join them and I'll call you when we're ready.

(Crow exits)

Daughter: Oooo! How exciting! Who's getting married?

Rabbit: Us.

Daughter: Whaaa … Huh?

Rabbit: Why are you looking so sad? The guests are all here and everyone is happy but you.

Daughter: But I don't want to get married.

Rabbit: Don't worry you'll get used to the idea. Now cheer up! I'm going to check on my guests.

(Exits)

Daughter: What will I do? What will I do? Wait- all this straw. I'll make a scarecrow and scare him.

(She exits into the kitchen)

Scene 4. Later in the Rabbit-Hutch.

(Enter Rabbit)

Rabbit: (Sees scarecrow) What are you doing sitting here? We're ready to start now, so you need to set all the food out and get yourself ready! What's the matter, got carrots in your ears? Hey! (He pokes the scarecrow with his finger and it falls over.) Ahhhh! She's turned into a scarecrow!

(Enter Crow)

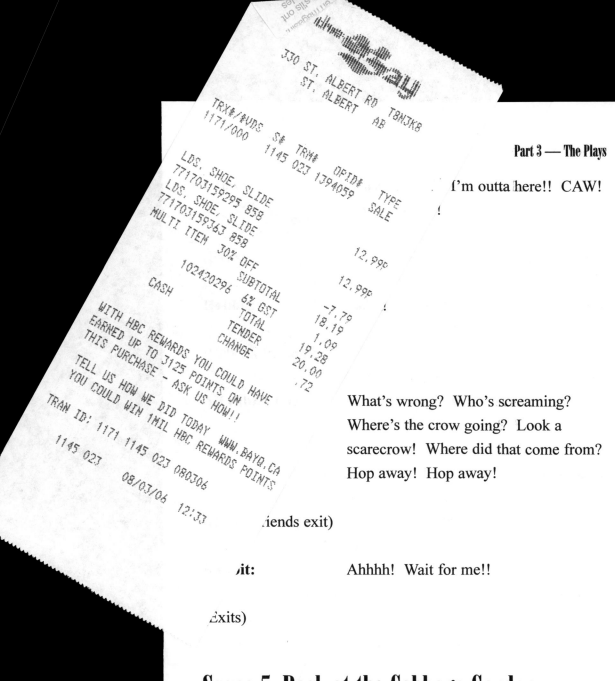

I'm outta here!! CAW!

What's wrong? Who's screaming?
Where's the crow going? Look a
scarecrow! Where did that come from?
Hop away! Hop away!

(...iends exit)

...it: Ahhhh! Wait for me!!

(...xits)

Scene 5. Back at the Cabbage Garden.

(Enter Mother)

Mother: Where is my daughter? She's been
                         gone a very long time. I hope that she

didn't have a problem shooing away the rabbit.

(Enter Daughter)

Daughter: Hello, Mother! How wonderful it is to see you again!

Mother: Hello, my dear. Where have you been? Did you have a problem with that rabbit?

Daughter: Well, yes, mother, I did, sort of … the rabbit invited me to a party at his hutch and I said okay. But the party wasn't quite what I expected it to be.

Mother: Well my dear, you know you don't always have to say "yes" to someone who asks you to do something. But, for being such a wonderful and helpful daughter I will make you your favorite treat: carrot cake.

Daughter: Uhh …That would be lovely mother, but if you don't mind could I have chocolate cake instead?

Mother: See, you're learning to say "no" already. Of course I'll make a chocolate cake, my dear. Anything you want.

(Exits)

Daughter: Thank you Mother. Ah. Home sweet home. Home is where the heart is. There's no place like …

Mother: (Enters) Coming dear?

Daughter: Oh yes, Mother. Sorry.

(Both exit)

The End!